Parenting the Christian Way

Parenting the Christian Way

Biblical Ideals to Augment
the Call of Parenthood

Athriba Sangtam

Christian World Imprints

First Published in 2020 by

Christian World Imprints
Christian Publishing & Books from India
C-3, Wazirpur Industrial Area
Delhi-110052
cwidelhi2017@gmail.com
www.ChristianWorldImprints.com
Phone: +91 11 41526079

ISBN: 978-93-5148-498-1

Printed in India.

Dedication

To my beautiful family
My wife Likhum and my kids Dori, Muwaza and Kehli
The most beautiful gift ever!
The inspiration to become a better hubby
and a dad derives from them

Forward

It is my pleasure to forward this well-timed resource book written by Athriba Sangtam, a promising scholar in the department of Christian Ministry specialized in Pastoral Counseling. Athriba's earlier book *Children Without Childhood* has a wide circulation and received appreciation from many serious readers. With great success of the first book and gaining confidence as a writer, the author is ready with another book, *Parenting the Christian Way: Biblical Ideals to Augment the Call of Parenthood* which is a comprehensive approach to parenting dealing with issues like-the joy of parenting, parents of the bible, principles of Christian parenting, disciplining children the Christian way, leaving behind spiritual inheritance, disadvantaged children of our times, spiritual nurturing, understanding a child, Spousal relationship vis-a-vis child development, partners in parenting, the grand role of grandparenting. Finally, the author proposes the need for pastoral initiatives.

A parent's duties to their children is being their role models and establish better relationship, to explain the purpose of life to them. In todays' world, children are becoming more and more bound- not liberated. They are becoming addicted to the internet, social media, mobile phone, new trends, and external appearances. These things are binding children to becoming consumers, celebrity fans and bricks in a social wall. They have become used to a sense of entitlement instead of responsibility and their life is spent mostly indoor. Indulgent parents let children rule their lives like kings and queens and it is not the school's fault, nor were they born like that. Occupational therapists by the drove are saying "the parents are to be held responsible." For what? For not being emotionally accessible to children.

Parents are also constantly being digitally distracted and they are not clearly defining limits to conduct. We are not teaching children to be responsible and we are not making sure they get enough sleep and balance diet. So as a result, among other drawbacks, children are in a devastating emotional state. Parenting in the context of all these complexities demands parents to seriously contemplate and reflect on the significance of effective parenting to make each child's life meaningful, purposeful, and successful.

With the fast pace of child theology movement inclusion in the syllabi of the theological courses and the Holistic Child Development programs gaining importance worldwide, this resourceful material will be of great help. I am personally longing to read it. I strongly advice Students, Pastors, Parents, Teachers and all people interested in the art of parenting to read this book.

Rev. Dr. Phanenmo Kath
Associate Prof. Pastoral Counseling &
Psychology and Dean of ILEMA, ETC, Jorhat

Preface

What a joy to be a parent! The joy of becoming parents and to witness our children mature each day is a joy we cannot trade for anything else. Not everyone have the opportunity to experience the joy of having and nurturing children of their own. People who are privileged to become parents are called to look at their position from a new perspective. Privileges always come with certain responsibility which has to be honoured. In fact, becoming a parent is not just a privilege but a very sacred affair. It is a sacred affair because our children are God's gift and the joy of receiving children as gifts from God comes with the responsibility to nurture them well. Any parent who looks at parenting from this perspective is indeed a blessed parent and their children will grow up to become persons of worth. The sad fact which cannot be hid is the fact that some parents have no or little clue as to how important parenting is not just for the children but also for themselves as parents. Many fail to understand the link that exists in terms of relating parenting both as biological and spiritual.

One of the most beautiful phase of one's life is the childhood; a phase that is filled with laughter and fun. Childhood has always been associated with innocence, purity of mind and soul but the plight of many children today proves it otherwise. The innocence associated with childhood has been marred by elements resulting in the absence of childhood in a child's life. Many children grow without knowing what it means to be a child. Many of our children today fails to enjoy their childhood and are growing up into 'Childhood Deprived Adults.' Childhood being the formative years of a person's life is vital for a healthy growth. The phenomenon of childhood deprived adult happens because of many factors where poor parenting tops the list. Parenting and issues related to childhood always goes hand in hand. They are inseparable.

God instituted marriage intending a man and a woman to come together and begin a family. Since marriage is instituted by God, everything that fall within the perimeter of a marriage is sacred. A family is an institution where love and peace reigns. It is a place where no one is a stranger and everyone is loved and appreciated. A glance at lives of many reveals a grim picture. There are families where the experience of laughter and peace is non-existent but strife and stress dominates. Some families rarely sit together at home not because they don't have time but because they cannot face one another. Some children hardly share any thoughts with their parents because of insecurity. God did not institute a family to live in such manner. When we see people being stripped away of their joy, we cannot afford to remain indifferent but be stirred.

No matter whether we are parents or a child; we are supposed to enjoy this phase. I sometimes contemplate how many parents derive joy and pleasure out their parenthood; how many children derive joy out of their childhood. Do we consider parenthood to be just a burden? Have we unconsciously passed on this message to our kids by not allowing them to enjoy their childhood? Issues related to parenting are multifaceted. "Many parents do not know their responsibilities; children innocently accept/follow what is being directed to them by their parents; governmental agencies and many non-governmental agencies try to fulfil their task just for the sake of sustaining their project; many church organizations fail to envision a holistic mission."

I have always considered pursuing this subject, viz., parenting and child development not just as a passion but because I strongly felt the need to address this issue. Parents struggling to nurture their children are real; Children struggling to grow up because of poor parenting are real. Expecting someone to lend a helping hand to teach them the art of Christian parenting is a dream for many. Children dreaming of somebody passing some parenting tips to their parents and restoring their childhood are real. I wish to be one among the many who wish to see those dreams being fulfilled and see smiles and satisfaction on the faces of both parents and their children. I wish to see parents and children walking around hand in hand as friends. I wish to see children sharing their thoughts to their parents without a hint of insecurity. I wish to witness parents celebrating their parenthood joyfully every moment of their lives. I can't do much to see all these dreams being fulfilled but I can definitely put my best foot forward and dream for something big happening in someone's family through my writings. This book comes to you infused with the most sincere prayer; a prayer to grant each parent the right spirit to becoming better parents to their children.

My heartfelt gratitude goes to Rev. Dr. Phanenmo Kath for graciously writing the "Forward" to this book; Dr. Daniel Tikhir, Dr. Tsüknungrenla and Rev. John Croyle for their kind act of endorsing my humble book. A special gratitude to my lovely wife who never hesitated to encourage and support me and of course making sure that our children to not distract me in the process of my writing. Finally Christian World Imprints deserves a big "Thank you" for making the publication of this humble book a reality.

Athriba Sangtam
Sept. 2020

Introduction

Parenting is a gift that comes with responsibility. The responsibility to nurture our children also comes with a special package which helps us to become effective parents. The special package is "joy." This joy that comes from God is something that is left for parents to claim. Parenting can become a wonderful journey of life with our children provided we claim the blessing of parenthood in its fullness. Claiming the blessing of "being fruitful" in its fullness is the focal point of the **first chapter** of the book.

People receive inspiration from various sources, sometimes unexpected too. Even when we are clueless about something, inspirations from various sources enable us to keep going. It is always a delight to be inspired by something/someone. The **second chapter** of the book is a collection of inspirational parents as well as parents who flawed in their approach as parents as recorded in the Bible. The inspiration we receive through reading their way of nurturing and sustaining their families will truly open our eyes towards becoming parents we ought to be. The flaws they committed will also enable us to be cautious as we carry out our parental responsibility today.

The bible is a resource book not just for parenting but for various other subjects. Christian parenting has to derive a lot from the scripture. In fact, the right tool for Christian parenting comes from the scripture. The **third chapter** of the book encompasses insights from the scripture which are framed as the principles of Christian parenting. There are Christian principles for parenting in the teachings of the Bible and these principles should guide us to become model of parenting that others can emulate. We do not live in a world adhering to a single culture. Every community adheres to their own unique culture. Even for parenting norms, something that is considered normal in one's culture is considered the other way round. Looking at parenting from a Christian perspective gives us a better prospect since biblical principles apply to all people (Christians) irrespective of race and culture. From a Christian perspective, the possibility of having a common set of norms for parenting becomes a reality.

In parenting, nurturing and disciplining goes hand in hand always. Parents and other care givers are mostly carried away when it comes to disciplining a child. Should we spank a child? Should we scream at them? Should we just let them do what they want? The norms of disciplining vary from culture to culture. In certain culture, spanking a child may be considered gross but some culture may permit parents to do it. What the scripture sanctions when it comes to disciplining is of utmost importance in this chapter. No matter what our culture dictates, Christian parenting must consider seriously, the norms of disciplining as sanctioned by the scripture. The bible definitely has answer to this quest and **chapter four** explores this aspect and also checks the danger of misinformed biblical truths being applied in our lives.

In many cultures of the world, the worth of a person is measured by the material possessions owned. A good father/mother is measured by the possession he/she leave behind to be inherited by the children. Every parents wish to leave behind something good for the next generation. This aspect is discussed as a separate chapter because of the dimensional difference. The rest of the discussion focuses on the parental role while living but this is an aspect that happens after they are far gone. This chapter focuses on the spiritual inheritance we can leave behind for our children. This is an aspect many ignore because it appears to be vague but the Bible tells us so. The material riches we leave behind as inheritance for our children matter less when compared with the unseen yet empowering spiritual inheritance. This **fifth chapter** enlightens us on how we can leave behind a Christian legacy for the next generation to follow which is categorically the richest inheritance one can ever leave behind.

Childhood is synonymous with innocence, laughter and joy but many children miss the opportunity to experience the joy of being a child due to various reasons. The sixth chapter of the book is an effort to penetrate into a world hidden from the normal sight. It illustrates the dark truth of how children are coerced as well as compelled to sacrifice their childhood. It portrays the world of 'the haves and the have nots' where some parents with silent tears let go of their children from their embrace just because of their poverty. The effect of the disparity of the society is seen in the tears of the poor. The truth of how some unscrupulous people can take undue advantage of another's poverty is presented in the **sixth chapter**.

The **seventh chapter** of the book stresses the incompleteness of Christian parenting without spiritual nurturing. It is a part and parcel of holistic parenting. Human beings are both mortal and spiritual beings and therefore nurturing our children in both these aspects is important. Many parents have completely left the role of spiritual nurturing of their children to the hands of the Christian education department of the church and forgot the preordained role of parents in contributing towards the spiritual formation of their kids. The nurturing received from the school, church and other agencies are important yet secondary. The task of nurturing is primarily endowed upon the parents. No other agencies can substitute the preordained responsibility of parents to nurture their children. Parenting is not just a biological phenomenon but a spiritual. Parents are called not just to be a biological parent but a spiritual parent too. Christian parenting cannot be considered complete with spiritual nurturing. It is a part and parcel of holistic parenting. Human beings are both mortal and spiritual beings and therefore nurturing our children in both these aspects is important.

Parents and care givers may experience dead ends in the process of parenting not because their children are extraordinarily bad but because they failed to understand the world of children. They failed to look at the world from the lens of a child. Many parents tend to ignore the world of a child and try to nurture them according to our worldview which will certainly damage our relationship with each other. Our worldview is completely different and to understand them require lot of patience as well as wisdom too. There are certain ways of understanding the world of children and **chapter eight** of the book attempts to assists parents and caregivers with certain aspects of exploring the world of a child.

Any discussion about child development basically circles around the role of the father and the mother. The **ninth chapter** of the book connects parenting with the relationship shared between the husband and the wife. As we talk of their parenthood, sometimes we may lose sight of the spousal connexion they share with one another. Before becoming a parent to somebody, they are in the first place husband and wife. The spousal relationship they share with one another in fact determines to a large extent the kind of parent they may become to their children. As we address issues such as Christian parenting, one of the key element is to address them as individual person first and further upgrade to levels of a couple, family and so forth.

The **tenth chapter** reconsiders the traditional concept of role distribution between the father and the mother. In fact role distribution has been misunderstood by many resulting in many spouses shying away from their responsibility and leaving the other half to manage the family which they themselves can do. This chapter introduces the model of compensation through which parenting can become partnership. Partnership in parenting is important because they are supposed to work together as a team from start till finish. One cannot back off and brush aside our responsibility in the middle of nowhere. When this model of parenting is applied, it is not even necessary to have role distribution based on gender. Both the husband and the wife share equal responsibility to manage the family.

As someone matures in age after successfully nurturing a generation, having the privilege to witness the birth of another generation and participate in their nurturing is no doubt a gift from God. Accepting the biblical view of becoming a grandparent can make it a joyful experience. It is not about retirement, aging or being unproductive. The bible takes the role of grandparents in nurturing their grandchildren to a new level. It is a definitely a gift but with certain responsibility. Every privilege comes attached with certain responsibilities. The **eleventh chapter** of the book unravels the beauty of grandparenting and how someone can enjoy grandparenting to the fullest.

The church has a big role to play in making dreams come to reality in the life of individuals and families. In a Christian context, the place the church hold is immense. The final chapter exerts the influence of the church upon the life of its members and ways to utilize this influence to the maximum. The teaching of the church should not just circles around the heavenly realm but should equally encompass other areas of human concern. There is much that the church can contribute towards nurturing families in the Christian way and a holistic ministerial framework is what is proposed in the **final chapter**.

Chapter 1

The Joy of Parenthood

"Joy is a gift within the gift of parenthood"

God Said, "Be Fruitful and Multiply"

After the creation of the first human family, God blessed them saying "be fruitful and multiply" (Gen. 1:28). Surprisingly, this blessing was never uttered to any of the created beings except to the one in whose image he created. Since then human beings continue to participate in the creative plan of God every time we procreate. To procreate is a gift from God thereby making it a sacred affair. "The procreation and nurturing of children is a reminder that the family does not exist for its own sake but in order to participate in God's ongoing creative activity."[1] It was on the sixth day after the creation of humankind

[1] Herbert Anderson, "The Family as a Context for Change and as a Changing Context: A Sign that God is Always Making Something New," *The Church and Pastoral Care,* edited by Leroy Aden and J. Harold Ellens (Grand Rapids: Baker Book House, 1988), 158.

that God declared with much satisfaction, "It was good!" (Gen 1:31). God is our parent and the delight of the whole creation activity culminates following the birth of the first humankind. What a joy it must have been! The joy and satisfaction that God experienced after the culmination of his creation account is what his created being, humans can experience as we partake the gift of his blessing to be fruitful and multiply.

The Gift of Joy to all Parents

One of the most significant things that can happen in somebody's life is the birth of a child. The moment we realize the birth of a baby is the moment when we become a different being. If being a parent does not change a person, what can? It is one of those special moments in life we can't trade away for anything. As we discuss the joy one derives from parenting, we must also consider that not everyone get the opportunity to become parents no matter how much one may wish to. Not everyone can experience the joy that comes out of parenting one's own biological child. Therefore, parenting can be considered a calling in the sense that only some can procreate. Yet this view does not inhibit the others from enjoying the joy of parenting. Those who cannot procreate due to physiological inability or other reasons can still enjoy this bliss in other ways to which God is generous enough. The inability to procreate should not be considered as a deterrent to experience this joy. The adage, "when God closes a door, he opens another" has a very close call to people in this category. Human's disappointing circumstances can become God's appointed moment to lead us towards experiencing a more profound joy depending on how willing we are to be led by Him.

Due to the tendency of humans to disobey the will of God, many have also turned this joy into gloom. For some people because of ill-fated circumstances, the joy of parenthood is turned into despair. For instance, the declaration of pregnancy by your partner before marriage, a woman getting pregnant because of a sexual assault committed on her is not a moment of joy. In situations such as these, it will be indeed very difficult to indulge in the bliss of becoming a parent. It is imperative to question whether becoming a parent through such circumstances deter him/her from experiencing the joy of parenthood? Irrespective of the circumstances we are called to parenthood, one must consider it a divine obligation to nurture the child and reap the joy of parenthood. Many innocent lives have been destroyed because of not considering it as a divine obligation to nurture the child. The societal dictates takes the upper hand in such situation. The circumstances which led to someone becoming a parent should not supersede the divine obligation to nurture the child. No matter the circumstances, every parent must be helped to enjoy the bliss of parenthood. Real joy comes from God and even in the worst situations of life we can still experience God's prescribed joy.

No matter how we become parents, be it through legal union, Christian marital union or other union, anyone can enjoy the joy of parenthood that comes from God. Every parent has the entitlement to enjoy this provision. There is no doubt that the child him/herself is a gift from God which is portrayed in Ps. 127:3 "Children are a gift from the Lord" but the joy of parenting is the other dimension of gift that comes along with the child. The irony is that many parents absorb themselves only in the glitches of parenting and miss the wonderful opportunity to unwrap this additional gift which should essentially sustain their parental journey. A gift is supposed to be unwrapped and appreciated. Possessing an unwrapped gift at home in the corner holds no value. Parents are called to accept the gift of a child as well as the gift of being joyful.

Joy Reinforces Parenting

What actually is this gift of joy? How can we possibly derive joy out of parenthood? John 16:21 records, "a woman giving birth to a child has pain because her time has come; but when her baby is born she forgets the anguish because of her joy that a child is born into the world." Listening to the first cry of the baby makes a mother forget the intense pain and struggle she goes through. The joy of holding the new born is magical and it eases all pain. The pleasures of seeing them play and giggle, take their first step, utter their first word is something which cannot be compared to anything. In spite of parenting being a challenging affair, parents who have deciphered the mystery of this joy can endure all challenges. To concentrate on the brunt of parenting or claim the joy that is derived out of parenting is a choice each parent will have to make.

Parenting is a very demanding affair. Many parents experiences stress, frustrations, burnouts and depression. For some parents, parenting is more of a hardship than bliss. Parents go through phases that sometimes steals away their joy and peace. Where do we go wrong? Are we in the right track? Apostle Paul mentions in 1 Cor. 10:13 about God providing us the provision that enables us to endure trails and not allowing us to be tempted beyond human endurance. This statement is made in the context of enduring trials and temptations yet a striking feature can be learnt from this statement that connects to our subject. If God provides us the needed reinforcement even to endure trials and temptations, will He not have arranged a reinforcement that is necessary for us to successfully "be fruitful and multiply"? The reinforcement that supports us in our journey as parents is not classified information. It is in fact the divine joy that comes from him. This divine joy is what keeps parents going no matter how challenging the task may be. Without this additional support, we are susceptible to defeat. Everything is set for us from the beginning. The moment God declared, "be fruitful and multiply," He understood human limitations and prepared a backup for us. We just have to claim and own it.

Joy: the Fruit of the Spirit

Joy is one of the fruits of the spirit as mentioned in Gal. 5:21, "but the fruit of the spirit is love, joy, forbearance, kindness, goodness, faithfulness, gentleness and self-control." We cannot compare the joy that comes from God to that of the joy we derive from the world. God's joy is a complete joy, a fruit of the spirit. A person who is not spiritual may not savour something that is spiritual. Deriving the complete joy out of parenting depends on the spiritual position of the parents since parenting is not just a biological phenomenon but a spiritual one too. Therefore, the real complete joy of parenting can be enjoyed only when we understand the duality of both the physical and spiritual. When parenting is viewed both as a physical and spiritual responsibility, the fruits of the spirits will be manifested.

God wants all parents to take over the responsibility of parenthood with much joy. He does not want us to consider it as a burden but a divine obligation. He has also the needed strength prepared for us as we encounter new challenges unfold before our eyes in the process of parenting. The moment we understand the truth behind parenthood we will joyfully endure anything. This does not mean that you will not face any difficulty credited to parenthood. There is no doubt that we will encounter different forms of challenges on the way. The only difference is that we will no longer face challenges in life like people who have no hope for support. We will instead focus at the brighter side and smile in the face of trails because we know who is in control. When the joy of parenthood fills our heart, every tear you shed for your child, every sacrifice you make, every obstacle that you face is always worthwhile. We will find satisfaction in every pain. If someone asks us why Christian parenting is unique? I guess we have the answer. It is summed up in the following sentences. "The gift of parenthood comes along with the gift of Joy. It is a gift within gifts which sustains people towards completing the task of being fruitful and multiply."

Allow yourself to fully immerse in the pure joy of parenting that comes from God. A hiccup now and then in the process of parenting is a normal thing yet do not be caught up in it and miss the opportunity to partake the gift of peace and joy in your life. God wants us to be happy and joyful even in the midst of adversities. Being joyful does not always mean the absence of pain and struggle but even in the darkest moment of life, there is joy for people who have learnt to claim the promises of God and walk along with Him.

Chapter 2

Parents of the Bible

"Allow the Bible to inspire you to become better parents"

A. Inspiring Parents of the Bible

Some people may consider talks about good parenting to be a creation of this generation. Some may go to the extent of considering biblical thoughts to have no relevance to anything beyond the religious/ spiritual exercise of the church. It is no surprise that Bible has resources to help humans find an answer in all their circumstances even in term of parenting a child. The Bible has record of some inspiring parents who considered parenting as a sacred responsibility and the examples they have set continue to inspire people towards a better understanding of parenting role that each parent must play today. Travelling through the biblical records, penetrating into the homes of some inspiring characters of the Bible and attempting to understand their philosophy of parenting is a unique journey each one of us can undertake. This journey will definitely right many wrongs that we may have committed in our quest to become a good parent. This journey will also enhance our theology/philosophy about parenting that we already consider to know.

Let us journey through the Bible and meet some unique and inspiring parents.

1. Joshua

Joshua who took over the reign of leading God's chosen people from Moses not only proved himself to be a dynamic leader but also proved himself to be an exemplary father. Against all odds, Joshua decided to abide with the commandment of God and declared, "But as for me and my household, we will serve the Lord." (Jos. 24:15). He has considered the spiritual development of his household a priority. A father taking over the responsibility of the family in living a life that pleases God is noteworthy in the famous statement made by Joshua. Joshua not only declares his commitment to God as a family but also challenges the tribes of Israel to make the right choice. Joshua cared less about what the majority cares but he did what was right. He set the perfect example of someone who is the head of the household; being responsible over his household. In our society, many fathers may shy away from such commitments and leave it to the wives and children but in this public declaration of faith, Joshua place himself first (...as for me and my family...) and his household and further encouraged his people to imitate him. He is the example of an ideal father who leads the family and society by setting examples.

2. Manoah

The bible records that Manoah and his wife were barren until one day when an angel of the Lord visited the wife and declared the blessing of a son to them and to follow certain dietary discipline. Manoah is a figure from the Bible whose prayer for wisdom to nurture his child has a lot to teach us today (Judges 13:8-12). On listening to the prayer, the Lord sent his angel again to instruct both of them. They are none other than the parents of Samson.

The relationship shared between Manoah and his wife and the trust they placed on God for the fulfilment of the promise is wonderful. Our children are God's gifts and we are to nurture them according to His standards. How many parents care to ask God to give us the right wisdom by which we must nurture our children? When Manaoh prayed, God answered and provided the required guidance to nurture their child.

3. Job

Job was a wealthy man who lived in Uz with his large family. He was considered upright and God fearing. The bible records how Job regularly offered burnt offerings to the Lord on behalf of his children for the sins they might have committed (Job 1:5). Job wished his children to be blameless in the Lord like him. Job understood what it means to trust the Lord and remain righteous in his sight. The parenting tip we can extract from the parenting role played by Job is important for us today. When parents are righteous, we cannot afford to lose our children to unrighteousness. Only when we have experienced the joy of living a godly life, we will wish our children to follow suit. Job is someone in the Bible who encountered the biggest fear every parent has: losing our children and property completely. Yet his trust in the Lord remained unshaken and he ultimately triumphs over the schemes of the devil.

4. Eunice

She was the inspiring mother of Timothy. The faith that has been passed down from a generation to the next generation is manifested in the life of Timothy. Apostle Paul commented Timothy's mother and grandmother this way, "I am reminded of your sincere faith, a faith that dwelt first in your grandmother Lois and your mother Eunice and Now, I am sure, dwells in you as well." (II Tim. 1:5). This is a testimony to Timothy's godly upbringing by the mother. She was a responsible mother who instructed her son Timothy in all matters related to faith which made Timothy become a prominent figure of the church in the nascent church (II Tim. 3:15). This is the influence a mother can have on her children which has a strong impact on the lives and future of their children. Timothy further joins Paul in his missionary travels (Rom. 16:21) and eventually become the pastor of the church at Ephesus (I Tim.1:3).

5. Hannah

Hannah is mentioned in the Bible as the other wife of Elkanah who was barren (I Sam 1:2-2:11). Hannah was depressed and sad but her weeping heart was not something God cannot see. She was humiliated by people around but her incessant prayer for a child continued. She promised God, "Lord Almighty, if you will only look on your servant's misery and remember me, and not forget your servant but give her a son, then I will give him to the Lord for all the days of his life and no razor will ever be used on his head" (I Sam: 1:11). God blessed them with a son whom they named Samuel. Hannah nursed him until the weaning period was complete and took him back to the temple and offered him to the priest for the service of the Lord. After surrendering her son to the service of the Lord, Hannah prayed and exclaimed, "My heart rejoices in the Lord..." (I Sam. 2:1). What a faithful mother! How many parents will find this occasion joyful? Can someone give away something that we have longed for a long time? Hannah did it. Her fervent prayer was answered by God and she in turn, surrenders her son for the service of the Lord. Fulfilling the promise in surrendering her son for the service of the Lord was considered more important than her emotional attachment with her son and furthermore, she rejoices in this act.

Recollect the stories of many other unnamed parents of the Bible who went beyond the social norms just for the love of their children. In Mt. 19 we have the record of some parents who brought their children in order that they receive the blessing of Jesus himself. They earnestly wanted Jesus to lay his hands upon their children and bless them. In spite of the social constrains the parents took the leap of faith for the love of their children. Remember that it was a society where women and children did not have the similar opportunity an adult male enjoy and that may be one of the reasons why the disciples of Jesus reacted to the act of the parents trying to reach Jesus. When Jesus sensed what was going on, he reacted in the most surprising manner. He said, "Let the children come to me, and do not hinder them..." The act of the parents circumventing the societal norms just for the love of their children resulting in the profound reaction from Jesus Christ is a beautiful illustration of parental and divine love for children. Jesus further uses the analogy of the innocence of a child to illustrate the Kingdom of God.

Inspiration Derived from Biblical Model Parents

1. **Seek and Study the Manual of Parenting**: We ask the Lord for many things including the blessing of a child. When our prayer is answered, we forget the one who gifted us our children. We forget that we need divine intervention to nurture our children. Our children are God's gift and they cannot be raised with human standards. Manoah and his wife did exactly what every parent should do in order to raise a child in God's standard. Every vehicle/gadgets comes with a manual of operation without which we cannot operate it well. Even for nurturing a child, there is a divine manual which every parent should be thorough with.
2. **Become a Role Model**: Parents should be role models as manifested by Joshua. Sadly, the opposite happens in the life of many families. Some parents force their children to do something which they will seldom do. The lesson learnt from the popular statement made by Joshua and its aftermath is that when we become role models, the rest follow suit. Joshua became the role model and allowed other to imitate him. He put himself first and his household in the service of the Lord.
3. **Become the Spiritual Support**: If misfortune can destroy a person, it will definitely destroy Job but the biblical account records how righteousness triumphs over evil. Job, the righteous man tried to become an unwavering spiritual support for his children. He stood firm as a 'prayer warrior' to defend his children from harm and to present his children righteous in the sight of God. Job was not just righteous but a man of unwavering faith. Our prayers should become the backbone for our children. Interceding for our children's welfare is the most beautiful expression of love.

4. **Leave behind Inheritance of Righteousness**: Lois and Eunice passed to the next generation not just a legacy of righteousness but a generation of righteous descendants, a generation of people of strong faith. The life and ministry of Timothy is an embodiment of the faith of Lois and Eunice. Their faith relationship with God did not end with their lives but they passed it on to Timothy through teaching by word and example. The relationship we share with God today should determines the faith of the next generation too. This is the beauty of our faith relationship with God. We have the privilege of passing it on to our next generation.
5. **Always Keep Your Promise**: A promise made to God is a sacred covenant and it should be honoured. We make promises of various kinds to God but the enthusiasm dies down once our desire are met. Hannah fulfilled the commitment she made to God even when it was the hardest thing for her to do. She gladly fulfilled her promise which gladdened the heart of God.

Christian parents must always look to the Bible for inspiration. There are enough resources in the Bible that has the power to inspire us towards becoming better parents. It not only contains stories of inspirational parents but also contains the divine mandate for parenting. A wise person will always appreciate the rich treasure the Bible hold for us not just for parenting but for every aspect of our lives.

B. Flaws Learnt from Parents in the Bible

Many attempts have been made to distort historical facts in the course of time particularly in case where some individuals/organizations wishes to drag certain historical facts to their advantage or when certain historical facts are too indecent, some may try to twist or erase it. Some historical facts are no more available in the history books anymore. It has just vanished somewhere along the way. The good thing about the Bible is it contains history from both perspectives. It contains records which show both side of the same coin. The Bible contains stories of inspirational parents as well as records of parents who did not fall within the perimeter of a good parent and messed up their parenthood. Some of the biblical heroes that we look up to failed miserably at one point of time as a parent. This section of the book attempts to revisit some of their homes and check for insights that will avert today's parent from committing the same mistake.

1. David

David is a biblical hero to many of us and his feats remains fresh till today. He was a man after God's own heart (I Sam. 13:14). Yet as a parent he was a man who was a passive father to his children. The nature of parenting he exhibited is manifested in the life of his children. His passivity resulted in sexual crime and murder within his own household. His eldest son Amnon sexually assaults his half-sister Tamar and Absalom avenge Tamar by murdering his brother Amnon. Had David initiated a more active role such tragedy would not have happened in his family. 2 Sam. 13:21 records, "…but he would not punish his son, because he loved him, for he was his firstborn." His failure to punish Amnon led to the development of hatred between Absalom and Amnon which lead to a murder. 1 Kings 1:6 further records, "His father had never at any time displeased him by asking 'why have you done thus and so?'" This record is in reference to David who never reprimanded one of his sons Adonijah. Adonijah further grew up and attempts to dethrone his father from the throne though he was not the rightful heir. David recourses to the same mistake when he restrain from providing justice to Amnon by punishing Absalom. Absalom in the later course of time rebels against his father and gets killed in a battle. Throughout David's parental journey we find it filled with Parent-sibling rivalry. We can only assume whether his own transgression of sexual immorality with Bathsheba and the subsequent murder of Uriah, the husband of Bathsheba drained away his audacity to correct his children. This failure also has a direct association to what is recorded in 2 Sam. 12:11. It says, "Thus says the Lord: I will raise up trouble against you from within your own house…" This declaration of the wrath of God was for David for the sins he has committed. David is one of the examples of a passive father in the Bible who failed to discipline his children and ends up destroying not only his family but the nation of Israel too. Solomon, one of the sons of David who succeeded as king of Israel him puts it this way, "Folly is bound up in the heart of a boy but the rod of discipline drives it away" (Pro. 22:15).

2. Eli

Eli was the High priest of Shiloh. He had two sons Hophni and Phinehas who were both priests of the Lord. The Bible records that these two sons of the High priest were scoundrels who had no regard for the divine profession they were called to. They engaged in mismanagement of the offering placed before God by the people of Israel (1 Sam. 2:12-17), indulged in sexual immorality (1 Sam. 2:22) and treated it with contempt (I Sam. 2:17). This act displeased the God whom they were called to serve. Eli tried to reprimand them (1 Sam. 2:23-25) but the prophecy that came for Eli's household through a man of God mentions that Eli honoured his sons more than God (I Sam. 2:29). This is an indication that Eli did not do enough to discipline his sons and bring them to the right track. The impending punishment reserved for Eli and his family as mentioned in the prophecy was appalling. The punishment included losing the longevity of life, poverty, be killed by sword, losing both sons on the same day. This punishment is incurred upon Eli and his household not just because the children were undisciplined but they choose to disregard the household of God. Eli himself said, "If one person sins against one another, someone can intercede for the sinner with the Lord; but when someone sins against the Lord, who can make intercession?" (I Sam. 2:25). In the battle between the Philistines and the Israelites, Hophni and Phinehas got killed and the Ark of the Covenant captured by the enemy (I Sam. 4:11). When the new of defeat of the Israelite's army, the capture of the Ark of the Covenant and the death of Hophni and Phinehas reached the ears of Eli, he fell backward from the seat he sat and died of a broken neck (1 Sam. 4:18).

3. Samuel

Samuel was someone who was chosen by God to succeed Eli as the High priest. He served the Lord under Eli and later succeeded him after his death. I Sam. 8 records that in his old age he made his sons judges over Israel. Unfortunately his sons Joel and Abijah did not follow his ways and engaged themselves in taking bribe and perverted justice. The elders of Israel were compelled to question the integrity of the position of Joel and Abijah as judges of Israel before Samuel and demanded a king to govern Israel. The disgraced name of Joel and Abijah no longer appears in the rest of the Bible. The position of the judges was never a hereditary obligation to perform and one does not have the authority to name a successor yet Samuel chooses to appoint his sons as judges over Israel.

Lessons Learnt from Parenting Flaws in the Bible

1. Disciplining our children is a must. No parent should be passive in the way they deal with their children. When children make a mistake we must correct them instantly and appropriately no matter how much we love them. One ignored mistake leads to another and it rarely stops. One's transgression can also become a hindrance to discipline one's children. David faced the same problem. From David's parenting role we understand that one flawed family can affect the whole community/nation.
2. The degree of discipline should depend on the nature of their mistake. Eli made the mistake of not considering the sins committed by his sons seriously. It was not just a minor offence but a transgression against God himself. A curse befalls upon the entire family.
3. As parents, the welfare of our children is always considered a priority yet we must learn to always seek and follow the will of God. Our priority may not necessarily be God's priority always. Samuel made the mistake of letting his parental instinct take over the law of the divine.
4. No matter how good and righteous a person may be, we may become an example of a flawed parent if we ignore the parental mandates necessary to succeed in parenting.

The bible is a complete book that inspires people who read it with an open heart and mind. No amount of reading can inspire us unless we are willing to open up and allow the Word of God to get dissolved in our being. Stories of successful parents as well as parents who failed at certain point of time recorded in the Bible are important cues for parenting that should inspire us to become better. Allow the Bible to inspire you to become a better parent to the children that the Lord has blessed you.

Chapter 3

Principles of Christian Parenting

"Go to the Bible. It elevates parenting to a mystical height"

1. Christian Parenting is a Sacred Responsibility

God blessed humankind and uttered his blessing, "Be fruitful and multiply..." (Gen. 1:28). When we become parents, we participate in the sacred mission of being fruitful. Children are gifts from the Lord (Ps. 127:3-5) and thus to nurture them and bring them up in the Christian standard is a divine responsibility. Joseph made a similar declaration when he introduced his children to his father. He said, "They are the sons God has given me here in Egypt" (Gen 48:9). Parents needs to reaffirms that our children belong to God and they are gifts from Him. The moment we affirm this truth, we acknowledge the involvement of the divine in the process of our parenting. The truth of parenting is that children come through us but they don't come from us. It is God from whom parents receive their child. To raise a child who comes from God/who belongs to God is indeed a sacred responsibility.

2. Christian Parenting is Qualitative Parenting

Anyone can become parents but to become parents of quality will need a better discerning. Qualitative parenting happens when someone understands and adheres to the biblical standard of parenting. The number of children we have does not matter; we may let them live in a mansion, provide everything they desire, send them to the best schools and universities but it does not matter much when it comes to qualitative parenting. The most important standard of measuring whether someone falls in this category is to examine the quality of the children he/she has nurtured. In the industrial and corporate world, the quality of their product is what determines the reputation of the company. Qualitative parenting is exactly the same. The quality of our children determines who we are or in another words we determine who our children will become.

3. Christian Parenting Raises a Godly Family

Deut. 6 has God's mandate to the people of Israel for raising children in God's standard. It is not just a mandate for raising godly children but a family. The people of Israel were on the brink of entering a new society and a new culture. God prepares them to hold the family together by holding fast to the decrees passed on to them. With the influx of new culture and traditions into our society, many of our children are dragged away from our fold and are lost. How important it is to teach our family the right values and help them stay strong no matter what circumstances they may face. While we cannot be perfect parent, we can be a godly parent, and that is precisely the kind of parent we should strive to become. Mother Teresa held that "peace and war begins at home." And she appealed to parents to "bring love into your home. If you love God, begin by loving your child, your husband, your wife."[1] Effective parenting does not

---

[1] Kathryn Spink, *Mother Teresa: An Authorized Biography,* (London: Harper and Collins, 1997), 133.

require perfection; it simply requires love, commitment, a sense of purpose, and a willingness to depend on God.[2] A godly upbringing is what will sustain them even as they venture out into the world. When godly values are imprinted into their hearts, it remains with them. We must understand that the forces of the evil is strong and convincing which should encourage us to instil in our children stronger godly values if we value the lives of our children and family.

4. Christian Parenting Focuses on Holistic Development

A detailed narrative about the childhood of Jesus is not found in the Bible yet the nature of development that Jesus Christ went through from a small baby to an adult is summed up beautifully in Luke 2:52. Luke records, "And Jesus increased in wisdom and in years, and in divine and human favour." The component of development mentioned in this text is interesting to note. Jesus grew mentally (wisdom), physically (in years), spiritually (divine) and socially (human favour). This holistic upbringing of Jesus not only prepared him for the divine task ahead of him but sets a divine standard of how a child must be raised. If a child was raised in this manner during the biblical times, does it not question the integrity of child nurturing we adhere to when we cannot even attain this standard in the 21st century. The holistic development of a child is what the Bible sanctions which is not just a concept but manifested in the person of Jesus Christ himself. Our children need to be empowered with all aspect of development in order to face the world.

5. Christian Parenting is Being a Role Models

What you want your children to become is what you should be. Becoming a parent is very easy but becoming a role model for our children is what makes parenting a challenge. Many parents are just good orators; they teach and set guidelines for their children to follow which they seldom follow. They want their children to go to church while they don't go. They want their children to restrain from being aggressive while they (husband and wife) fight over small

---

[2] Bob and Ann Livesay, *Parenting Edition,* (Nashville: Freeman-Smith, 2007), 9.

matters. They want their children to become the best but they can never be the best father/mother to their children. Children imitate the character of their parents. What we are is who they will be. In the simplest term, being a role model is to show them in words and deeds how you want them to be. Role modelling is about loving our kids like the way Jesus love us. Jesus followed his father's example and we are taught to follow Jesus and in the similar way, we must become role models for our children to follow (John 8: 38, John 13:15, 1 Cor. 11:1).[3] The most proud moment for a parent is not when your children pass an exam; not when they sing in the choir but when they can say with utmost pride, "I wish to become like my mom and dad!" Children may consider pop artists, actors and so forth that they may have never met or known personally as their role model. They try to imitate their lifestyles and personality. Imagine ourselves as parents becoming a role model for our children with whom we have the privilege to spend time every day. The impact of parents becoming role models for their children is immense.

6. Christian Parenting Uses God's Word as Tools

Christian parenting must derive its insights from the word of God. Christian parents must seek the resources available in the Bible and apply them in their lives. Every wisdom and knowledge of the world and beyond comes from God alone. God gave us an instruction manual for life which is the Bible. There are parents who take this gift for granted and try teaching their children without consulting the handbook.[4] Parenting models such as 'Christian parenting' are never possible in the absence of dependency on the word of God. A family that is rooted in the Word of God is in fact what Christian parenting is all about. A family that promotes dependency on the word of God and claim its promises never drift apart and the bond they share with one another is the portrayal of the bond they share with God.

---

[3] Tom and Chaundel Holladay, *Love Powered Parenting, Loving your Kids the way Jesus Loves You*, (Michigan: Zondervan, 2011), 87.

[4] John Trent, Rick Osborne, Kurt Bruner, *Parent's Guide to the Spiritual Growth of Children: Helping Your Child Develop a Personal Faith* (Illinois: Tyndale House Publishers, 2000), 29.

7. Christian Parenting Consider Each Child Unique

The tendency of the parents to ignore the goodness and focus on the weakness of our children can be very disastrous for many children. The comparison that parents make between siblings and friends has never proved to be helpful for a child to perform better. Each child is unique and therefore not all of our children will be in the same scale. Some may prove to be very studious, disciplined, and helpful but some may not attain the standard that we have set to be considered a good child. One may be good in certain area but parents do not have to place him/her in a position that makes the other children feel devalued. There is no harm in appreciating someone's goodness but in the process the other should never be neglected. Strengths are to be affirmed in each child and in the process of affirmation their strength, their weakness must also be addressed.[5] Each child possesses something good in them. We must identify them, appreciate it and also their weakness be corrected in the right manner. If we just appreciate the good and ignore the bad, we contribute towards making them worse. Unconditional positive strokes are what keep people going. Parents should restrain from creating yardstick that lifts up someone and in the process devalues the other. Each child should be unconditionally accepted as they are and made to feel unique.

8. Christian Parenting Makes Time for Each Other

Many tend to blame the fast paced world as the reason why we cannot be available for one another. We have created a world where we are made to think that we hardly have enough time to pause for a moment and take a deep breath. Members of the family hardly spend quality time with one another. I wonder how many families find it difficult to share a dinner together with all the members present around the table at the same time. This is not just because we are too busy but we cannot manage our time well. As individuals, we need a break for ourselves as well as for our family members. The quality time we share with one another make the familial bond stronger

[5] Charles F. Boyd, *Different Children Different Needs: The Art of Adjustable Parenting*, (Oregon: Multnomah Publishers, 1994), 147-148.

and intimate. Being available to not necessarily mean being present physically but it involves a holistic presence. It is both a physical, emotional, and mental availability to one another. Look out for opportunities to spend quality time with one another as a family. A family that spends quality time together stays together! In spite of the "busy schedule" we are committed to, we should create a strong tradition of spending quality time together as a family. It will prove to be a therapeutic experience for all members. In fact, the productivity outside the family affair too will improve as a result of the quality time spent with the family. A balanced spousal relationship is also a must for parent-child relationship and this relationship can be enhanced by being available for one another.

9. Christian Parenting Creates a Child-Friendly Home

It is said "home is where the heart is." Basically a home is made up of parents and the children. The elements that establish a home determines whether or not it is a child-friendly home. A child-friendly home is basically a home where he/she feels loved and welcomed. It is a place where he/she experiences no prejudice and judgment. It is a place where he/she loves to spend time without feeling of insecurity. It is a place where he/she can both laugh and cry but deep within, he/she know that he/she is special. Each Christian home should become a sanctum for our children to grow. A child-friendly home does not necessarily mean a home with tons of toys and goodies; it can just be a simple home, even without toys but a home where a child can be him/herself. Since the early family life lays the foundation for later personal, social adjustment or maladjustment, the effect of specific home conditions on child development obviously are important.[6]

10. Christian Parenting Abhor Favouritism

In the bible, Isaac and Rebecca are parents who displayed favouritism. Gen. 25:28 records, "Isaac loved Esau...but Rebecca favoured Jacob." This favouritism led to a serious problem in the family of

---

[6] Louis R. Thorpe, *Child Psychology and Development,* 2nd edition, (New York: The Ronald Press Company, 1946), 382.

Isaac and Rebecca. It created a serious strife between the siblings too. Parents must love their children equally no matter who they are. Display of favouritism by parents has never achieved anything good. The enmity developed between Esau and Jacob should be a strong example that can happen in anyone's family when elements of favouritism exist in the family. Every single child should be showered the same level of parental love. Letting the children understand that they are equally loved is very important. Elements of favouritism in the family not only create hatred towards parents but also create sibling rivalry. If the concept of, "our parents love you more" exist in the family, parents must remember that we are sowing seeds of hatred and strife. Once this take root, sibling rivalry goes a long way and is quite difficult to control later. The first instance of sibling rivalry as recorded in the Bible is between Cain and Abel although it does not indicate to its origin being poor parenting. The characteristic of jealously is in fact a part of human characteristic yet in most of the people it is tamed. According to James Dobson, this attribute is manifested beyond control when parents compare their children unfavourably with each other.[7] Parents must therefore be cautious about not provoking sibling rivalry by encouraging positive vibes and a spirit to respect differences at home.

Creating a family that is based on biblical values will be the greatest achievement parents can ever achieve. The primary environment for the development of children is the family. Therefore, the values that the family adhere to are very important. The treatment a child receives at home is reflected in their dealing outside.[8] Home environment is the most important setting that either shapes or distorts a child. Biblical principles of parenting are resources in the Bible which will prove to be useful only when we apply it. Such values will cease to be valuable if we don't apply it. A diamond is useless when it is allowed to be covered in dirt and ultimately forget. Though it is valuable, it ceases to be valuable

---

[7] James Dobson, *The Strong Willed Child: Birth through Adolescence,* (Illinois: Tyndale Publishers, 1984), 128-129.

[8] Lakshameshwar Thakur, *Child Development and Psychology*, (New Delhi: Centrum Press, 2015), 216.

when people do not wear diamond jewellery anymore. It ceases to be priceless, when it is covered in dirt and trampled upon. Its worth depends solely based on how people value and utilize it. Christian parents must adhere to and manifest these biblical principles in their lives and family. God has gifted parents the responsibility of nurturing a child. God has also blessed humans with instinct, intellect and wisdom to understand the responsibility assigned to us. We must utilize every resources available be it the Bible or any other healthy source to augment the sacred parenting role given to us.

Chapter 4

Disciplining Children the Christian Way

"The most important ingredient of disciplining is love; without it you just punish"

The Need for Disciplining

The need to train and discipline children when they are in their formative years is very important and the Bible has a direct reference to this subject. "Train a child in the way he should go, even when he is old he will not depart from it" (Pro. 22:6). Nurturing children depend on the culture of a particular context. In some cultures of the world, we notice a very authoritarian nature of disciplining while some culture may have a softer approach to nurturing. In some culture, spanking and other disciplinary method is a normal phenomenon while it is not so in other context. Something that is considered right in one context is considered the opposite in another. Trying to understand ways of disciplining children may be very challenging because of the different approach one may use as per the dictates of the culture one belong to. Therefore, the need to understand the biblical mandate for disciplining a child is important because no matter which culture or context we belong to, the biblical mandate apply to all Christian parents. The bible has a lot to teach us about the importance of disciplining children the Christian way. Heb. 12:5-11 sums up the whole concept of Christian disciplining.

> ...My son, do not make light of the Lord's discipline, and do not lose heart when he rebukes you, because **the Lord disciplines the one he loves**, and he chastens everyone he accepts as his son. Endure hardship as discipline; God is treating you as his children. For what children are not disciplined by their father? If you are not disciplined-and everyone undergoes discipline-then you are not legitimate, not true sons and daughters at all. Moreover, we have all had fathers who disciplined us and we respect them for it. How much more should we submit to the father of spirit and live! They discipline us for a little while as they thought best; but God disciplines us for our good, in order that we may share in his holiness. No discipline seems pleasant at that time but painful. Later on it **produces a harvest of righteousness and peace** for those who have been **trained** by it."

The summary of the above extract is "Disciplining with Love." The comparison to the disciplining received from an earthly parent and our heavenly Father is presented here. The extract ends with a note about producing "a harvest of righteousness" which is a by-product of "disciplining with love." Disciplining has its way and when it is channelled properly, the end result is beneficial but disciplining the wrong way will produce adverse result. Disciplining is also not punishment but it is a "training." Some parents assume that punishment is discipline. Discipline and love are inseparable and they are not two separate entities while punishment is just a small part of discipline.[1] The concept of disciplining changes when we connect out disciplining as a way of training our children in the right track.

The formative developmental years of a person is one of the most important phase of one's life. What they have been taught as a child remains with them and it further develops into their adult personality. The bible affirms the fact that the nature of nurturing received as a child remains with the person even when old (Pro. 22:6). Eph. 6:4 further mentions "...but bring them up in the discipline and instruction of the Lord." This is a mandate no Christian parent should dare to ignore; bringing up children in the discipline and instruction of the Lord. Christian parenting should not be just a by-product of the scientific, psychological and other disciplines but it is about nurturing child as per God's standard. All the derivations from other fields of study are summed up in the texts of the Bible which are cited everywhere in this book. Nurturing children as per God's standard is the mandate given to Christian parents. Trying to identify God's standard for nurturing our children is the fundamental aspect of Christian parenting.

Misinterpreting Divine Standard of Disciplining

The bible has its own standards of disciplining children. The biblical standards of disciplining children has been misinterpreted which has led to widespread abuse of children for the sake of discipline. Many children are found to be at the receiving end as parents and caregivers satisfy their ego and carnal pleasures. One of the most common references from the Bible that has been misinterpreted is, "spare the rod and spoil the child..." (Pro. 13:24). This has resulted in the prevalence of corporal punishment in school as well as homes. This biblical text has been used to justify the punishment meted out to children by parents and other caregivers. In fact, these standards have been considered only at the face value. The bible does not sanction punishing our children to the extent of causing physical, mental and psychological harm. Proverbs 13:24 further mentions,

---

[1] D.Ross Campell, *How to Really Love Your Child* (Colorado: Life Journey, 2003), 88.

"he who loves their children is careful to discipline them." How many parents punish their children out of love? The problem with parents and other caregivers is that punishment is used as a means of venting out their anger and frustration on their children but not with the intention to discipline them. Discipline does not always necessarily mean punishing them. Punishing them may control the immediate misbehaviour but it does not do well with the child's long term personality growth. Sharp verbal reprimand and physical force is warranted when children engage in behaviours that need to be stopped immediately because they child may harm himself and others too but any form of punishment that denigrate the child's worth as a person are never justifies.[2] On the other hand, a child learns to be violent when his/her every mistake is responded with violence. Punishment is always understood as a means to bring about obedience but it is essential to realize that discipline enfolds the responsibility of the parents to mould the child by encouraging/ rewarding good behaviour and correcting unacceptable behaviour. Parents should see discipline as a nurturing tool and set clear limits for behaviour. Along with disciplining, constant and consistent love, praise and encouragement lead the child to adopt more acceptable pattern of behaviour. Sadly there are many parents who fails to appreciate their children when they do something good but become visible only when they do something wrong. Many fail to appreciate their children but are always available to point out their mistakes in life. Many cannot spend quality time with their children but quick to be judgmental when their children fail in life.

Hard Facts of Christian Disciplining?

1. Do we regret after punishing our kids (eg. after spanking)? If we answer "yes", I am afraid we did not do the right thing. The reason may be because we punished them due of our uncontrolled anger, disappointment, and frustration and so forth. The bible never sanctions us to punish our kids because of our anger but we are asked to discipline them with love. When we do something out of love we will not regret. I Corinthians 12:4-5

[2] Laura E. Berk, *Child Development* (Boston: Allyn and Bacon, 1989), 510.

explain the attributes of love this way, "love is patient, love is kind…it does not dishonour others…it is not easily angered…" Disciplining children out of our anger does not fall within the biblical mandate of disciplining children. Love should be the only motivation to discipline our children.

2. Do we resort to corporal punishment as the only means of disciplining our kids? The word 'discipline' is synonymous with 'violence' (verbal/physical) for some parents which will prove to be detrimental for the parent-child relationship as well as the personality growth of the child. Disciplining can happen even without use of corporal punishment. Sometimes, the only tool required to discipline a child is a simple hug, a stroll in the park, appreciating the small deeds they do and so forth. The concept of "An eye for an eye" is definitely not what we wish our kids to learn but they will surely learn it if we do not hesitate to punish them every time they do something wrong.
3. Do we have the courage to genuinely say "I am sorry!" when we commit something wrong in the presence of our kids? Children learn from us and they will learn to express apology when they make mistakes. This will avoid many confrontations in the family between parents and kids. In fact disciplining has to begin from us.
4. Do we reward or bribe our kids? Whether it be in the kid's world or the adult world, bribing can never be considered morally right. Parents sometimes confuse between this two-bribing and rewarding. When we pop a candy into their mouth while they create a tantrum, it may be considered a bribe. A child is fed with the notion that creating a tantrum results in receiving goodies from the parents. When a child is provided a candy for being obedient it is considered a reward. In both the cases, it involves just a candy yet the end result of the latter is healthier for the child. The child is made to understand that good behaviour results in reward. Christian parents should reward their children not bribe.
5. Are we consistent and firm in our parental approach? A "yes" should be a yes and a "No" a no. In some cultures, there are statements which we use on our kids such as, "I will break your

leg if you go there again, I will tear off your ear if you don't listen, I will skin you if you do this..." Are we really serious when we pour out these phrases upon our kids as a part of disciplining? Parents actually intend to frighten them into not doing something but the intended objective shall never be achieved because we may easily verbalize it but seldom follow it. Since we don't carry out what we say, our kids will continue to do what they do. It is best to avoid derogatory phrases in our disciplinary approach and set achievable standards which we can consistently and firmly follow.

6. Does your parenting style builds or break? (Eph. 6:4/Col. 3:21). "Do not embitter/exasperate your child" is what the two biblical references states. There is a danger of making our children more aggressive, resentful and reckless just because we fail to be responsible. We must learn how to deal with children age appropriately. We must learn to deal with them reasonably. Our children are not robots that are programmed or designed to perform in certain way no matter what. The form of parenting style we apply may do more harm than good if we are not cautious.

Disciplining our children is not an option but a necessity and it is intended to allow our children grow the right way. Disciplining them in the proper manner will definitely have a positive impact in their lives while disciplining them improperly destroys them. The process and objective of disciplining has been misunderstood and it has proved to be quite detrimental to the holistic growth of children. Imagine a scenario-a certain man cut down a tree because it prevents the sun rays from entering his compound. Discipline is instruction or training designed to correct misbehaviour, and develop the disciplined one. It does not involve justice, punishment, or getting even. Punishment is a penalty inflicted on an offender as retribution. Punishment has justice as its goal, not reformation or personal growth.[3] Many are led to believe that these two words mean the same thing but it isn't. The problem is with some translation of

---

[3] Bruce Narramore, *Help! I'm a Parent,* (Michigan: Zondervan Publishing House, 1972), 40.

the bible where these two words are used interchangeably. Imagine another scenario-a certain man in order to enjoy the warmth of the sun trims some branches of a tree since it shades the sun. These two scenarios illustrate two types of disciplining; the former is the type that harms the one who is disciplined and the latter is the one where both parties benefit. The agenda of these two men is the same but the approach differs. Our disciplining should not destroy but recreate, redirect and replenish.

Chapter 5

Leaving Behind Spiritual Inheritance

"The greatest gift you can leave behind is a strong spiritual legacy"

The spirituality that we profess should not end with us but the scripture teaches us to pass on our spiritual inheritance to our children. Deut. 4:9-11, 6:4-9, 11:18-21 records the instruction given by God to the people of Israel to teach their children everything about the goodness of the Lord. Eph. 6:4 and Col. 3:21 address parents regarding child nurturing in the discipline and instruction of the Lord. It also signifies a parenting role that should be derived from God's ways of taking care of His children. We always want the best for our children. We struggle to nurture, educate, and provide everything possible to let them grow well in every possible manner. Many parents always go the extra mile for the sake of their children. The care and nurturing we give them when we are able is seldom considered enough. Many dream of leaving behind material inheritances for their children. This chapter does not undermine the tradition of leaving behind material possessions for our children but attempts to underlines a perspective of leaving behind inheritances that is holistic in nature. I consider many things important when it comes to the welfare of my children. One day when I am gone, I wish to leave behind lots of properties, enough money in the bank and a well settled business establishment to sustain them. The list will definitely go on but to leave behind spiritual inheritance will normally not occur in my mind. Even when it does, it will occupy the second place. The bible instructs us that the one we consider secondary should be the priority. "My child, keep your father's commandment, and do not forsake your mother's teaching" (Pro. 6:20) is the parents' spiritual obligation to guide their children in the path of spiritual truth. Parents have a biblical directive to instil in the child a desire for spiritual truth at a young age. "Train up a child in the way he should go; and when he is old, he will not depart from it" (Pro. 22:6). What we teach them today will sustain them even when they are old. Long after we have passed away, the legacy we leave behind will sustain them.

This perspective proposes leaving inheritances that include both material and spiritual but the latter takes the precedence.

1. What Do You Want Your Children to Inherit From You?

The love of parents for their children is something that is not understood unless one becomes a parent. Everything that parents do is ultimately for the welfare of their children. No parents wants their children to lack in anything during their lifetime as well as when they are gone. People indulge in buying huge properties and other monetary investments which ultimately can be inherited by their children. Even before parents pass away, wills are made and inheritances are shared between children and other members. Society tends to give undue importance to the materialistic inheritance. The Bible teaches us about leaving something else far more important than the material inheritance which is the spiritual inheritance. Mt. 16:26 have something to say about this- "what good will it be for someone to gain the whole world, yet forfeit their soul? Or what can anyone give in exchange for their soul?" It does not say that material goods are not good but in our quest to satisfy the worldly whims, we should not neglect the spiritual aspect of our life-our soul. No

Christian parents will want their children to wallow in riches but the soul far from being saved. The biggest and the greatest inheritance that we can leave behind for our children is the spiritual inheritance. The other forms are equally important but secondary. All the glory, fame and possession we have acquired during our lifetime will be left behind when we die. Our children will also one day bid adieu to this world but the good news for Christians is that this system can be reversed. If we have nurtured them well and leave behind a rich spiritual legacy, our children will follow us till heaven long after we are gone. We will surely bid good bye to all our worldly possession but our children can remain our eternal possession.

2. Do You Have What You Wish to Give Them?

We can give nothing to anyone when we don't have anything. We can only give when we own something. Some people inherit properties and other riches from their loved ones who have passed away. This is possible because the deceased possessed those riches and it has been passed down to them. If the deceased was a poor or a careless fellow, the story may be the opposite. Some family members end up paying the debts of the deceased who may have incurred it during his/her lifetime. Every parent may not be in a position to leave behind rich inheritances for our children but biblically, spiritual inheritance takes the precedence. It is a biblical mandate for each parent to nurture our children spiritually in words and deeds and leave behind a strong spiritual legacy for our children to follow. We should remember that unless we have it in us, we cannot set an example for our children. We should own it first before we pass it on. If we want our children to be disciplined, we should first be disciplined. Likewise if we want our children to grow in the likeness of Jesus Christ, we should be parents who live accordingly. A child cannot keep the father's commandment if the father does not have any commandment to keep; a child cannot forsake the mother's teaching if the mother does not have anything to teach her child. Parents should provide their children certain moral and ethical standards to live by. Many wish their children to live a good moral life and they know that it is the right thing to do but the irony is that they do not have the audacity to teach their children something they do not practice.

3. How Will You Leave Behind Spiritual Inheritance?

Children always look up to their parents for everything. Everything that the parents do will be imitated and therefore, helping our children to follow the right pattern of life through our words and action is a must if we care for our children's future. Titus 2:7 mentions, "In everything, show yourself to be an example by doing good works..." Parents need to live out their faith in order that their children develop their faith. Children need to see their parents living out their faith in deed and not in words alone. When we just preach to them and never live it out, children create an unrealistic concept of spirituality. Children are a gift from God. The remark made by Joseph while presenting his sons to his father says it all, "They are my sons, whom God has given me here" (Gen. 48:9). The moment we consider our children as a gift from God, the perspective of taking care of them completely changes.

We live in a materialistic world and therefore as parents cannot avoid thinking about the material aspect of inheritance that we can leave behind for our children. Yet as Christian parents, we should also take solace in the promises of God in the scripture about setting the priorities right. "Seek ye first the kingdom of God and his righteousness and all these things shall be added unto you" (Mt. 6:33). This is a wonderful promise about providence to be bestowed upon people who seek his kingdom and his righteousness. When we become people who seek him; when we nurture our children into people who seeks him, the material blessings just follows. It is a by-product of our relation with him. This is the reason why leaving behind spiritual inheritance is more important than material inheritance. This is insight is also encouraging for parents who are disheartened due to the fact that they are not in a position to leave behind material inheritance. Parents who have nurtured their children well and left a strong spiritual influence for their children to follow have in fact left the richest and the greatest inheritance for their children. As promised, God will not leave our children go hungry and naked as long as they continue to seek the kingdom of God. We shall have to boldly claim this promise of God for our children's future.

Chapter 6

The Disadvantaged Children of Our Times

"A child who fails to enjoy the bliss of childhood is a disadvantage child"

No child has the privilege of choosing the circumstances where he/she should be born. Fate decides what happens to the child. Some are born into rich families and some are born into broken and poverty-stricken families. People may tend to consider those who are born into rich families to be advantageous than those born into broken, poverty-stricken families. We are wrong. The social and economic circumstances of a child do not make him/her better than the rest of the peers. The disadvantaged children of our times belong to children that come both from the rich and the poor families, educated and uneducated, religious and the non-religious. No matter what their social, economic and religious state may be, the disadvantaged children are those who cannot experience the joy of childhood due to varied reasons. There are so many reasons that can prevent a child from experiencing real childhood. Any child who fails to experiences the joy and the bliss of childhood is a disadvantaged child.

Check how being on the advantage/disadvantaged is not determined by the socio, economic and religious state of the child in the table mentioned below. Comparing examples mentioned in column one with column two makes it clear that disadvantaged children can be produced from any type of family circumstances.

Table 1: The Disadvantaged Children of our Times

	Column One		Column Two
1	Some poor parents are coerced to send away their children with false promises of education, good salary, minimal household chorus etc and their children end up as a slave.	1	Some parents do not have time to spend with their children thereby letting their children find solace in TV, computers, cell phones, etc. They become slaves to gadgets.
2	Some parents do not have resources to buy toys for their kids. The kid grows up feeling the pain of insufficiency.	2	Some parents have enough resources to buy toys and fulfil every wishes and whims of their children. Finally, a pampered child!
3	Some illiterate parents cannot help their kids to complete their homework and let them struggle by themselves.	3	Some literate parents can help complete their kid's homework and make every decision for them.

The above table is an indication of how children are disadvantaged irrespective of their socio economic background. It is imperative for us to understand that any hindrances that prevent children from enjoying their childhood will prove to be a fatal blow to their holistic growth. Everyone wants their children to grow up in whole not in parts. This should not end just as a utopian dream but the dream to see a better maturity has to be sown during their childhood.

Elements that Disadvantages Children

1. Poor Parenting

Parenting is a challenging role. The irony is that many parents do the wrong thing with the right intention. In another word, they do not know what they do. Parents can sometimes be caught up in traditions which may not apply to the need of context. A requisite academic qualification is never required to become a parent and therefore, we cannot expect every parent to have knowledge about child nurturing. Many parents basically depend on their instinct to raise their kids as well as utilize the dos and don'ts that springs forth from one's own culture yet parenting has always been an overwhelming challenge for many. Parents are confused as to what is the right approach to the need of their children in today's context. Poor parenting is the primary element that can place children in the disadvantage. We see frustration and disappointment in the eyes of many parents. In spite of all the effort that they put in, nothing seem to work and many end up considering themselves to be a failure. Another group of parents who ends up jeopardising their children's growth and future are passive parents who do not care much about how their children grow. Passive parents lack the motivation to become better parents and do not consider the aftermath of their passivity on their children's future.

2. Poverty

Poverty is a real issue in our country. The reasons may vary from region to region but the pang of poverty is the same everywhere. Poverty prevents parents from sending their children to good school. When parents cannot afford to provide even a single decent meal for the day; school supplies, toys, gadgets, treats, new dresses is only a dream for children who are from a poverty ridden family. Finding a bottle of clean drinking water, a coin somebody may have dropped; leftover food somebody discarded is a big treat for many. Children from this background struggle so hard. They have big dreams but very small possibilities. They miss many opportunities to have fun, laugh and play like their other peers just because they are poor. Most of the children who are victims of the unscrupulous individual/gang belong to the disadvantaged section of the community. They understand it well that the child cannot fend for themselves nor can their parents/ guardian. Children in their innocence coupled with poverty-stricken parents/guardian faces a world so indifferent. For a handful of rice, a little sum of money, the promise of better education, they are coerced to trade their innocence away and they begin their struggle to survive the unforgiving world everyday of their lives while their advantaged peers enjoy the bliss of childhood in the loving bosom of their parents. There are individuals and organizations trying to help uplift such children and community. In the similar way there are people who take advantage of their insecurities and lure them with false promises which are rarely fulfilled. These children end up paying the price.

3. Lack of Adequate Parental Impetus from the Church

Every parent does not have proper knowledge about child nurturing. In fact no prerequisite academic/professional degree is required to become a parent. The church has a major role to play in providing the right parental impetus for them to become better parents. The church is responsible towards the task of nurturing the family since each family is an important unit of the church. The affirmation of the holistic responsibility of the church is imperative. No church will be stable unless the families that constitute the church are stabilized. It is encouraging to see some churches deeply engaged in this area of ministry. Trainings for fathers/mothers, young couple, seminar for children in different age group have become a part of the regular ministry of some churches. A sermon or two about parenting in a year does not meet the need of the people. A more professional assistance towards parenting is required. It is very difficult for someone to declare "I need help" but truth be told, parenting is a responsibility where every parent need help at one point of time or another.

4. The Demand for Minor Domestic Helper

Many homes have extra hands to assist the running of the family and most of those extra hands are minors. When we see the scenario of having helpers at home, most of them are not 'extra hands.' They are the 'main hands' that keep the house running. Many people prefer to have minors as helpers at home because of their innocence and simplicity. They are easily controlled as compared to an adult. Some fortunate minors land up in good and considerate families; receive proper education and other treatments. Some less fortunate minors ends up broken beyond repair. The joy and satisfaction; the hurts and despair that children go through are permanent. Most of the minor come from rural regions, broken families, and from poverty stricken families. Parents and guardians send their wards to live in another's house with the dream that their wards will have a better life. No parents will wholeheartedly send away their kids to live in other's house unless it is their only option. We can just imagine the sleepless nights the parents may go through, the memories of their kids in every nook and corner of their humble house, the innocent laughter and screams of every kid in the neighbourhood reminds them of their children who are far away from them just because they cannot support. The frustration of not being able to educate and support one's own children can be so overwhelming. Initially, many talk as if they wish to become the guardian angel to the helpless child but as the child reaches their homes, they do not consider it a sacred Christian privilege to take good care of them but manipulate this privilege.

5. Less Public Sensitization of Child Right/law

The existing laws related to safeguarding children and their rights may not have penetrated into the minds of the people in every section of the society. People may sometimes engage in things that are against the law without knowing that such a law exist. Many legal provisions are available for safeguarding the rights of children. Affordable legal assistance is also made available to the general people but many are ignorant about it. The concerns on child's right expressed by the United Nations Commission of Human Rights which is a set of international standards and measures intended to protect and promote the wellbeing of children in the society, the rights of children guaranteed in the constitution of India and the protection and care of children under the Juvenile Justice Act are something that each citizen must know. Civil organisations, student bodies and NGOs in many regions have also set up cells that monitors the system of employing minors but people tend to bypass such system and this is another reason for the plight of children being unheard in many cases. CHILDLINE India Foundation, a project of the Ministry of Women and Child Developments caters to children in distress. Many may not have heard or know the helpline which they can use to assist a child in need of assistance. As long as the 'extra hands' in every home is monitored, the level of harm on them will drastically reduce and timely intervention can be done.

The Task of Rousing up an Indifferent Society

Parenting isn't easy but the harder task to overcome is facing an indifferent society around us. We have become an individualistic society where nobody cares what everybody does. We live in a world of our own and care less about what happens outside our world. Parents have to struggle not only with the upbringing of their children alone but also face an indifferent society: a society that is silent and insensitive to the plight of people around them. We see children being subjected to inhuman treatment around us but many choose to remain silent. We see parents struggling to nurture their children but many choose to remain a silent spectator. Apart from being a mere spectator, is there a way we can participate in creating a world where the laughter of children fills the air, their innocent smiles brightens the day, and their carefree play last until exhaustion and parents enjoy their parenthood? Every one of us can be a part of this great cause. The lives of many children have been saved with the timely intervention of individual/group by informing the right agencies about children at risks and these examples should become catalyst to encourage us towards participating in this cause. There are governmental and civil agencies that strive to render the much needed help to children at risk. The least we can do is to support this cause. There are religious organizations and other civil entities that have considered this a struggle not only about their own children but a struggle to make this world a child friendly world.

Once upon a time we were a child; today we are parents. We should never forget that we have stood where they stand today. A glance into the past should bring memories of accomplishment as well as memories of failures as a child and a parent. Each one has begun our life as a small child. Nothing on earth can move a person if s/he is not moved by the tears of a child in distress; one is literally blind if s/he cannot notice the sadness in the face of a child; One is never full when s/he cannot notice the pang of hunger in a child's eye; we are never alive when we can destroy someone's childhood without a heart. When you notice a parent struggling to become the parent he/she is meant to be, never laugh it off but just remember that you have been there.

It is our responsibility to create a society that allows children to live and grow like children; a parent to enjoy their god's gifted parenthood. Society should appreciate and support efforts made by individuals and organization towards making this world a better place.

Chapter 7

Spiritual Nurturing

"The dual affiliation of a person to both physical and spiritual entity requires parenting to be both biological and spiritual"

Christian parenting cannot be considered complete with spiritual nurturing. It is a part and parcel of holistic parenting. Human beings are both mortal and spiritual beings and therefore nurturing our children in both these aspects is important. The dual affiliation of a person to both physical and spiritual entity requires parenting to be both biological and spiritual. When a child is born the physical affiliation is through and parents further are endowed the responsibility to link their spiritual affiliation at an early stage. In simple sense it means to set the foundation of their spiritual development timely. The spiritual foundation of your children's upbringing should be learning and applying God's truth in every area of life.[1] With the introduction of Christian education as a department

[1] John Trent, Rick Osborne, Kurt Bruner, *Parents' Guide to the Spiritual Growth of Children: Helping Children Develop a Personal faith* (Illinois: Tyndale

of the ministry of the church, the churches run the Sunday school and other children related programs in the church. Many parents have completely left the role of spiritual nurturing of their children to the hands of the Christian education department. This is a not a question about whether the Christian education department is doing enough for the spiritual nurturing of the children enrolled but it is a question about the preordained role of parents in contributing towards the spiritual formation of their kids. The nurturing received from the school, church and other agencies are important yet secondary. The task of nurturing is primarily endowed upon the parents. No other agencies can substitute the preordained responsibility of parents to nurture their children.

What Qualify a Person to Become a Spiritual Mentor?

The biggest hurdle for many parents is the question about their competency level for this task. Some parent may consider themselves to be incompetent to participate in the spiritual nurturing of their children. Does this task require a degree in theological education? Some may say that this aspect of development should solely be handled by the church. Why should parents be a part of this? What exactly is spiritual nurturing anyway? These questions must be answered to help parents understand their preordained task of spiritual nurturing.

This task does not necessarily require a formal theological degree yet this view does not undermine parents who are theological trained. The fact is theologically trained people does not spontaneously become spiritual parents. Some parents with formal theological degree may perform no better than someone who is not formally trained. This role is basically to be recognized as a preordained task assigned to all parents. We are not called just to be biological parents to our children but a spiritual parent too.

> Deut. 6:5-9, "Love the Lord your God with all your heart and with all your soul and with all your strength. These commandments that I give you today are to be on your heart. Impress them on your children. Talk about them

---

House Publishers, 2000), 50.

> when you sit at home and when you walk along the road, when you lie down and when you get up. Tie them as symbols on your hands and bind them on your forehead. Write them on the doorframe of your houses and on your gate."

This commissioning begins with a call to parents to "love the Lord your God with all your heart and with all your soul and with all your strength." Anyone who has this commandment imprinted on their heart qualifies to become a spiritual mentor to their children. To love God does not require any formal training and degrees; it is a personal relationship. No other texts in the Old Testament sound as direct as Deut. 6:5-9 when it comes to the parental task of the spiritual nurturing of their children. The task of spiritual nurturing is summed up in this text. Spiritual nurturing is not a one-time event but a continuous process and it encompasses the entire household. It does not end with a prayer being said in the evening. The task of nurturing does not finish with an admonition being said at one time but a constant nurturing is what is asked for from parents. The importance of nurturing the future generation spiritually was stressed even during the biblical times. Generation after generations, the people of Israel were sustained by God. God continued to sustain them due to the fact that they were his chosen race. Yet another fact is that the people of Israel never allowed the truth about the sustaining grace of God to eventually fade away in history.

In the New Testament, Eph. 6:4 records, "Fathers, do not exasperate your children; instead bring them up in the training and instruction of the Lord." This is way beyond fulfilling the responsibility of providing food, clothing, shelter, education, security and other needs. It is a commissioning of parents to become spiritual mentors for their children. The efforts of parents to nurture will be in vain unless this aspect becomes an integral part of the nurturing process. 1 Thess. 2:11, Paul elucidate the role of a spiritual parents when he said, "for you know that we deal with you as a father deals with his own children, encouraging, comforting and urging you to live lives worthy of God, who calls you into his kingdom and glory." This point to the fact that encouraging, comforting and urging them to live lives worthy of God is a very important spiritual task of parenting.

Essential Elements of Spiritual Nurturing

1. Spirituality is Best Exhibited Not Taught!

The best form of teaching is to become a model of what we teach and preach. This aspect is elucidated in John 5:19, "...very truly I tell you, the Son can do nothing by himself; he can do only what he sees his Father doing, because whatever the Father does the Son also does." This text is not used originally in direct reference to parenting but the essence of Christian parenting is visible in the text. Children learn from parents and what they do is what their children follow. This is the elementary perquisite for a successful spiritual nurturing of our children. Children naturally look up to their parents and therefore, whatever they see their parents exhibit is what they will imitate. It is not generally what we teach but what we exhibit that catches their attention the most and the future course of action is to imitate us. When children imitate us, do not consider it as weird. In fact they are programmed to do it. It is how they are programmed to mature. It is imperative for parents to be every cautious about this aspect and become role models for their children to follow. How a parent relates to a child has a direct bearing on how the child will relate to God.[2] It is very easy to ask someone to do something but difficult to say, "Do as I do." Exhibit spiritual maturity in the way we live and they follow suit.

2. Only What You Have is What You Can Give

Before commissioning parents to spiritually nurture their children, the scripture commissions parents to "love the Lord your God with all your heart and with all your soul and with all your strength" first. Deut. 6:6 records, "these commandments that I give you today are to be on your heart." It further mentions about passing it down to their household. It requires that the statutes of the divine should first be imprinted in the hearts of the parents first and passed on to the rest

[2] Cleveland Mc Donald and Philip M. Mc Donald, *Creating a Successful Christian Marriage*, (Michigan: Baker Books, 1994), 191.

of the household. One cannot really give to others what they don't have. They can give only what they have. The spiritual values that we want our children to inherit must first become our possession. Unless we possess it our children cannot inherit it. This pursuit of nurturing children with Christian values ends the moment we realize that we don't have it. This realization can also be the dawn of a new beginning towards becoming a mature practising Christian which will rewards us with the audacity to nurture our children spiritually.

3. Spiritual Nurturing Begins Right from Infancy

Some parents may make the mistake of ignoring spiritual nurturing of their children considering that it should be done only when they are matured enough. In fact, spiritual nurturing can begin as early as infancy. There are certainly age appropriate methods of nurturing which should not be ignored too. It is understandable that infants and toddlers cannot understand concepts that are abstract in nature yet faith is a feeling for them. The trust they develop when they are in your arm, the love they see in your eyes, their needs being fulfilled with care is the beginning of faith formation. They later develop this feeling into more mature faith as they continue to grow. The foundation of their faith is built at a very young age and parents should never miss this opportunity. Faith development should be a spontaneous process that should start right from infancy till death. Everything we do to a child, even infants and toddlers is to be understood as a means of spiritual development. Many have the notion of, "they are kids. They understand nothing." The task of parents and caregivers is nothing less than to introduce our children to God and God to them. Our children may be kids today but the nurturing they receive sustains them and ultimately helps them make their personal choice to follow God's direction at the right age they become accountable.[3] The way a person develops and matures is a fascinating process. Since we are adults, we think like an adult and assume that children learn like the way we do. It is a completely different process and depending on the age of person

---

[3] Timothy Jones, Nurturing a Child's Soul, (Nashville: Word Publishing, 2000), 100.

different approaches is required. Parents also should not be too eager to let children embrace their faith because as a child the faith that they exercises is not faith in God but faith in their parents. Our responsibility should be rather focussed on creating a loving, caring and spiritual environment.[4]

4. Set a Tradition of Having Family Moments

We live in a world where we create "busy schedule" and in our pursuit to fit into the busy schedule, we lose sight of the priorities of life. Upholding the values of this world and trying to fit into the system of the world become the priority for many people. If we are to evaluate the "rewarding moments" we spend outside of our home with the rewarding moments we spent at home, I guess we will all be surprised with the result. Some may realize that they have hardly talked to the spouses and their children. Some may even realize that their family members have become more of a stranger than people outside with whom they interact every day. Creating rejuvenating spiritual moments with our family is also a part of healthy family growth. It is not about creating a big formal religious event but a simple prayer together before a meal (I encourage family to eat meals together), a family fellowship/bible study at least in the weekends/ everyday (encourage the children to participate), attending worship service in the church together etc., are moments that keep a family together. Many cultures of the world have the tradition of narrating bed time stories to their children. Bible stories can be read to children as bed time stories. As a child many of us have experienced mesmerising moments listening to stories being narrated by our elders beside the fire place and we remember those stories even now. Children love listening to stories and the bible has wonderful stories which are way better then reading a fairy tale. As far as possible it is best to avoid making family moments too formal but with a bit of creativity such events can become exciting family moments which every member can look forward to. Both young and old love creative activities and are easily bored when things become too monotonous.

[4] Tim Kimmel, *Legacy of Love: A Plan for Parenting on Purpose*, (Oregon: Multnomah Press, 1989), 59-60.

We should also be cautious of the objective of such family moments. It should not be just to spend time together but a time of spiritual rejuvenation for the family. It is no surprise that the best spiritual development happens at home and not outside.

5. Set a Monthly Theme for the Family

You will witness more spontaneity in implementation of the values when we practice the method of following a theme for a certain period of time. For instance, a simple theme such as "kindness" can be set for a specific month. Parents may introduce the chosen value and help the children understand how they can put into practice this value in their daily lives. Encourage the members to exhibit this value within and outside the family throughout the month in their own creative way. At the end of the month, the family may set aside a time for a review at home or even outside of the home. Each member must be given opportunity to express how faithfully they were able to uphold the chosen value for the month. After the review is done, the family can celebrate over a dinner and also decide on the next theme for the following month. Such practical steps may help our children appreciate Christian values better in their life. We not only teach them but also create the opportunity to put into practice the values we hold so dear. The prolonged exposure to the practical implementation of the values will have a stronger effect on them.

6. Present the Gospel in Children's Language

The message of the gospel is relevant to all contexts but using irrelevant language may hinder the process of understanding it. Children will find it difficult to understand abstract and deep thoughts. The Christian doctrinal thoughts will never get into their mind but confuse them. Age appropriate language/phrases must be utilized to make the gospel simple and understandable. For instance, to a toddler, a simple "be kind to others" may make better sense than any well-defined theological though. Parents must be keen to teach themselves ways of upgrading their approaches as their children grow. The hardest experience may be with the first child. Once we get used to it we will easily keep pace with the rest of our kids. The volume of the input parents/caregivers invest does not matter as long as it is not age appropriate. Dealing with children in regard to the teaching of the gospel requires a simplification of our language without simplifying the truth of the gospel. In another word, use simple language to help them understand the gospel. Theological jargon must be avoided at all cost. This is not only to be applied while dealing with children but in other contexts too. Preachers are theologically trained and theological jargons unconsciously become a part of our language but the congregation are people who may have no idea about what we are blabbering about. While dealing with children, do not expect your child to start preaching a sermon; say an elaborate prayer and other stuffs like that. They will learn it in their due time as long as we create the right conducive environment for them.

Chapter 8

Understanding a Child

"In order to understand a child, look at him through the lens of a child"

The way a child relates to things as compared to an adult is different. As parents and caregivers, it is imperative for us to understand who a child is. Without understanding the way they perceive things, it will be a futile attempt to parent them. Many parents experience tough times not because their children are extraordinarily bad but because we fail to see the world from the lens of a child. A normal adult can decipher things that are abstract but a child will never understand things that are abstract because he/she understands and perceives the world only in concrete terms. The major mistake parents make in their parenting role is to deal with their children as they would to an adult. The bible records in record 1 Cor. 13:11 a contrast in the thought process between a child and an adult. "When I was a child, I talked like a child; I thought like a child, I reasoned like a child. When I become a man, I put the ways of childhood behind me." A child's mind is a crystal ball where nothing is hid. When they wish to cry, they cry; when they are sad, it is expressed on the face; when they feel sleepy they doze off anywhere; when they like/dislike something, they express it. An adult may restrain his/her emotions depending on the context and pretend to show interest even when not interested. It is a completely different world we share with our children. It is imperative for us to understand this special world before dealing with them.

Ways to Understand Children

1. Identify their Stages of Development

No one is born as an adult but a small child. It is natural for everyone to go through different stages of development. Each stage has its own hurtles which one must successfully accomplish. These stages that children go through must be understood in order that parents deal with them accordingly. Parents must be keen to help our children pass each stage in the manner they are supposed to advance. As a child, deal with them like a child; as a teenager, deal with them like a teenager. Likewise an adult be treated like an adult. No matter what their developmental stage may be, they will remain our child yet we should never withhold from them the right to individual self. Many parents make the mistake of ignoring their children's developmental stage and try to make their kids into 'geniuses.' Human developmental stages are exactly like the schooling one goes through. We upgrade from nursery to university phase by phase/class by class. Our children should not be burdened with anything beyond the limit of their physical, mental and emotional state. Erik Erikson opines that children should not be rushed in their development; that each developmental phase was vastly important and should be allowed time to fully unfold or dire emotional harm would be done, harm that would seriously undermine a child's ability to succeed in life.[1] For any normal child, eventually, they will go through each developmental stage. Our task is to help them advance each stage successfully. When parents understand their child's developmental

---

[1] Erik Erikson, *The Life Cycle Completed.* Extended version, (London: W.W. Norton & Company, 1997), 15.

stages, they will be able to facilitate the right impetus that will aid in their developmental process. Even toys come with advices in the packets/label stating the specific age group it is meant for. When we go against such advices/warnings, we risk harming our children though we purchased it because we simply love them. In simple term, the right impetus should be provided at the right time.

2. Communicate with Your Children

Communication is vital for building up a relationship. Clear communication between you and your child is essential for helping to improve their behaviour.it requires a lot of taking and listening.[2] Unless we communicate, we will never know their feeling. Let them learn to communicate their feeling to you. Sometimes unconsciously we discourage them to communicate with us. We need to ask questions that open up their emotions. Many parents are judgmental in our relationship with our children and this attitude will destroy our relationship with our kids. When we are judgmental, they will fear to share their problems with us. In your relationship with your kids, if you notice that your kids remain silent in your presence; consider it as a sign that your relationship with them is not right.

3. Spend Quality Time

Spending our time with them may sounds very simple and easy. We may stay together in the same house, eat the same food prepared in the same pot, see each other everyday but we may still drift apart from one another. It is not just about spending 'time' but it is about spending 'quality time." There is a big difference between these two concepts of spending time. Quality time does not necessarily mean spending the whole day together every day. In today's world, time is considered a luxury which many cannot afford yet if we value our family, we should set aside moments which can be spend with our family in the most productive way. Quality time is spent when we use it to explore one another's feeling, connect better and most

---

[2] Lynn Clark, *SOS Help for Parents: A Practical Guide for Handling Common Everyday Behavior Problems*, 2nd ed. (Kentucky: Parent Press & SOS Program, 2003), 15.

importantly enjoy and appreciate one another's presence. Spending quality time together brings up together and makes the familial bond stronger. You may afford to buy expensive toys and gadgets; you may take them on expensive vacations but this does not necessarily strengthen the bond unless you have spent quality time with one another. A simple stroll in the park, a picnic, playing a game, sharing a dinner is all that matters as long as it is spent well. It is simple things in life that matters most. The missing ingredient of parent child relationship today is not being able to spend quality time with one another. An hour of quality time spend with one's children is far better than spending the whole day with one's children without emotional attachment.[3]

4. Be Observant

Observation is keen to parenting. Sometimes we may tend to submerge ourselves in the hassle of parenting and forget to be observant. They may not tell us but they will not hide their emotions from their face and behaviour. Always look out for clues that make them behave different. Being observant also means to listen. Listening involves both our ears and eyes. When you listen using these two senses, you will definitely be aware of even the slightest abnormal behavioural change happening in your child's behaviour. When they are aggressive, find the reason that led them to be aggressive instead of trying to reprove them. When they lose their interest in studies, find out the reason instead of forcing them to study. Parents who are observant will have the benefit of identifying issues at the right time and nip it in the bud. The adage "A stitch in time saves nine" goes well with being observant. Sadly, many have lost their loved and dear ones just because they failed to be observant to the behavioural change happening in their lives.

[3] Athriba Sangtam, "Traditional Child Care Practices Among the Sangtam Nagas," in *Nurturing Children in the Tribal Society of North East India: A Search for Values*, edited by Razouselie Lasetso, I Toshi Jamir and Woba James (Jorhat: ILEMA, 2014), 277.

5. Spread their Wings

This sounds like a fairy tale but we are always astounded with the uniqueness and the level of creativity each possesses. The moment when they exhibit their true self is when we create the right environment to spread their wings. By letting them explore their creativity, we get to understand their unique qualities, their likes and dislikes, and their true self. In a restricted environment, they are restrained to be themselves and get no opportunity to explore themselves. Having children is almost like receiving a wrapped gift box. Unless it is opened we will never know what is inside. Parents should create time and space at home where they can be themselves and we just have to watch our children unfold their true selves.

6. Become a Child Yourself

Imagine yourself taking a stroll and you notice a child with a toy gun pretending to shoot at you. No doubt you will definitely hold your chest exclaiming "ahhhh…" and pretend to fall down. There are moments in the process of our parenting, when we have to become like a child. Becoming like a child not only helps the child connect with us but in fact it is helpful for us too. The moment we forget to be a child is the moment we stop growing. It is always beneficial to find time to sit and play with your kids, race around in the rain, roll around in the playground, and engage in all childish pranks not matter how stupid it may seem to an adult. There is a need to become like them to understand them well. These opportunities are fleeting moments which is not static. A day will come when we will be too old to engage in such activities and by the time we realize, our children will no longer be a child anymore. Precious moments like these when utilized well become not just sweet memories but agents that bond parent-child relationship.

Chapter 9

The Spousal Relationship vis-à-vis Child Development

"The quality of spousal relationship defines the quality of their child"

Any discussion about child development basically circles around the role of the father and the mother. As we talk of their parenthood, sometimes we may lose sight of the spousal connexion they share with one another. Before becoming a parent to somebody, they are in the first place husband and wife. The spousal relationship they share with one another in fact determines to a large extent the kind of parent they may be to their children. As we address issues such as Christian parenting, one of the key element is to address them as individual person first and further upgrade to levels of a couple, family and so forth.

In Gen. 2:24, we understand that when marital union between a man and a woman happens, they become one in body. This truth is further affirmed in Mt. 19:4-6, Mark 10:6-8 and

Eph. 5:30-32. In fact it is not just a physical union but a spiritual union too because marriage is instituted by God himself. The kind of relationship husband and wife should share with one another is categorically mentioned in Eph. 5:21-33. It is a physical as well as a spiritual union where both the husband and the wife complement each other. In the Old Testament too, we have texts such as in Hosea 1-3, Isaiah 54 and 62, Jer. 2-3 and 31, Ezekiel 16 and 23, Malachi 2:12-17 where reverence towards marriage as an institution is mentioned. Understanding how a husband and a wife should relate to one another in marriage is very important for the next challenge ahead of them which is the nurturing of their children. Unless one shares a good relationship with the other spouse, the rest of the task ahead is going to be in a mess. Some may get married filled with utopian dreams and such dreams are rarely fulfilled because marriage is between two mortals with human limitations. The nature of relationship they share with one another is not only vital for them but most importantly, vital for their children whom they are entrusted to nurture. Paul D. Meier expressed his conclusion about the root cause of many problems faced by children. The problem does not always stems from them but from parents. The treatment of most problems in children almost always involves helping the parents learn better way to live and love.[1] It is surprising to know how the relationship shared between spouses affect the growth of one's children. The quality of spousal relationship determines the quality of their children.

Elements of Spousal Relationship that Impact Children

1. Marriage that is Built on Love

People may unite together in marital bond for many reasons but the strongest reason that brings two people and sustains them together is love. Apart from love, no relationship survives. Even if it survives, it is never worth surviving unless there is love. A Christian family should be based on the foundation of love and nothing else. This is important not just for the sake of the couple but equally important

[1] Paul D. Meier, *Christian Child–Rearing and Personality Development,* (Michigan: Baker Book House, 1977), 18.

for the sake of their children. No force ever known to the human kind can match the power of love. This power has sustained marriage since the beginning when Adam and Eve unite as a couple. Blessed is a family that is built on the foundation of love! What a privilege when children are nurtured in home that is built on love! What a joy when children are nurtured by parents who recognize the power of love! If someone's marriage is consummated for any other reasons other than genuine love, the most important ingredient is missing. It is never late to identify and establish the marital relationship based on love. Marital bond like any other bonds must be renewed again and again. 1 Cor. 13:1-8 has the most beautiful description of the power of love (…love is patient; love is kind; love is not envious or boastful or arrogant or rude; it does not insist on its own way; it is not irritable or resentful; it does not rejoice on wrongdoing, but rejoice in the truth. It bears all things, believes all things, hopes all things, and endures all things. Love never ends…) A marriage that is built and nurtured based on this love is the most beautiful marriage on earth.

2. Expression of Love

People express love to one another in so many ways. Some can be very expressive and some don't. Children's first impression about love is derived from the love shared between the parents. Love is expressed both in words and deeds and parents should be very cautious in their relationship since they are the perfect example of a healthy relationship. How the father and the mother talk to one another, how they treat one another is important for children. Let your children know that you love one another in words and deeds. Constantly remind one another with, "I love you." Our expression of love should be spontaneous and it should come from the heart. For people who for reasons best known to them finds it difficult to express love in words, do it in deeds. Show that you care and love them by doing things that pleases them. Your children should learn what true love is through the love relationship you share with your spouse. Let them learn how you face each challenge together through the way you work hand in hand. "…while every early learning experience a child has is vital to his or her development as a person, we believe that the awareness of a deep, expressive, and passionate, love between the mother and father is the base upon which everything is built."[2] If a challenge is to be initiated by you for your children, ask this simple question to yourselves. Would you want your kids to find a life partner who will treat them like the way you treat you spouse now? If you hesitate to agree, it means that you will have to consider checking the relationship you share with your spouse.

3. Respect One Another

In a marital relationship, respecting one another goes far beyond than what we normally know about respect. Normally, we may understand respect in terms of revering a higher authority but in human relationship respect goes beyond this understanding. There is always a danger for a married couple to gradually lose the spirit of respecting one another. They may not quarrel and fight but disrespecting one another may happen in various forms. One of it is the failure to appreciate one another's effort. The golden words, "thank you, please, I love you, I missed you…" gradually fades away in time. Marital bond brings two individual together as a family and they are supposed to work as a single unit. Considering one another's opinion in performing tasks for the family is a form of respect. Many couples make the mistake of doing things, of course for the good of the family but without consulting the other half which unconsciously demean the other half. When you think together the opinions may differ but the best part is "You thought about it together!" The meanest form of disrespect to one another is when you scream and shout at your spouse in the presence of your children. Respecting one another also mean that you understand each other's limitations and accept it. It also means that you understand each other's dreams and aspirations. It can further go to the extent of remembering birthdays, anniversaries and other important events. Creative people do not actually wait for birthdays/anniversaries alone to surprise each other. Instead of

---

[2] Floyd and Harriet Thatcher, *Marriage for a Lifetime,* (Illinois: Harold Shaw Publishers, 1995), 149..

waiting for a specific day they create special moments by themselves and surprise one another.

4. Allow Yourselves to Grow Together

Two individuals united together by marriage are no more individuals but one. In a healthy marriage there is no such thing as "the husband is growing but the wife isn't." They need to grow together as a couple and as a family hand in hand. Anything that does not grow is not alive but dead. A family must be "alive" and each of the members contributes towards the growth. In the word of Paul Tournier, "as soon as husband and wife have the courage to be completely open with one another, whatever the cost, their marriage becomes once more a wonderful adventure."[3] Normally an adventure is something we would never plan with a complete stranger but always with friends and family whom we know and trust. Marital relationship is an adventure of trust and confidence that they can undertake together. A husband and a wife allow themselves to grow when they trust one another, confide with each other, and create a nurturing environment. When the right environment is created, they not only grow together but help one another grow and become a better person. One of the reasons for stagnation in marital life is because they fail to create an environment that is conducive for them to grow together.

5. Adhere to Christian Virtues

Christian couples must be different from the rest of the people. They should become a couple who radiates Christian virtues. The tag 'Christian couple' should resonate Christian values that can sustain marital relationship and the family. Their children should have the privilege to learn Christian values from them since their parents are Christian couple. A Christian family without Christian values is no Christian family at all. We live in a time where, new cultures have crept in into our families and hold an imperious influence in the family. It is okay to appreciate new cultures for the good that it

[3] Paul Tournier, *The Adventure of Living,* (New York: Harper and Row, 1965), 67.

unveils for people today but that does not give us the license to do away with Christian morals from our family. Christian virtues must always be the priority and the most important ingredient that should strengthen the marital bond the couple share and further sustain the family. Even when one of the partners is a little weak, one must encourage each other towards maintaining Christian values in both their personal as well as marital life.

6. Check Your Temperament

A marital relationship even when built on love is not always smiles, hugs and kisses. Two distinct individual trying to sustain together as a family is not easy. There will always be times of disagreement and misunderstanding. There are always forces that challenge them every day of their lives. Maintain a healthy interaction in the face of trails is the biggest challenge for many. Many people easily lose their cool and that is the moment when they interact with each other as an "individual" not as a wife/husband. Restraining ourselves from not interacting with one another as an individual should not be confused with respect for the individuality of a person. Respecting the individuality of one's spouse is important but interacting with one's spouse as an "individual" is a different thing. Both at good times and bad times, we should be husband and wife not individuals. The irony of marital relationship is that many remain husband and wife only at good times but become "individuals" at bad times. The moment you interact with one another as an individual, you tend to raise your voice and become violent. Remember to always interact with one another as a husband/wife. Most importantly, remember that your children are in the corner of the room trembling with fear listening and watching the drama. One must never argue and fight over any issue in the presence of their children. At least for the sake of your children, one should control one's temperament. When children witness violence at home, they may come to accept this as a normal and acceptable behaviour of family life. They also suffer from an array of behavioural, emotional and cognitive problems.[4]

[4] Sibnath Deb, *Children in Agony: A Source Book,* (New Delhi: Concept Publishing Company, 2006), 15.

7. Maintain the Same Yardstick for Disciplining Children

There is an illustration about a father who was very strict in giving pocket money to his children. Unless he is convinced about their need, he rarely provided money to his children. The twist in the story is whenever the father refuses to give money to the kids; the mother will discreetly provide money to her kids and further make the children promise not to let their father know about it. These are situation that will have a negative implication upon the way children think about their parent's disciplinary measures. A married couple may discuss and plan so many projects for their family such as family business, building projects, holidays, and children's education but may rarely discuss about maintaining a common yardstick for disciplining their children. Cases of confusion may arise when the father says "no" but the mother says "yes.' This confusion may lead the child to receive a wrong message that the one who denied him/her is not fair because the other parent agreed to the demand. This will pose a serious question in the mind of our children; when one can agree, why can't the other? It is imperative for parents to sit down and discuss the yardstick they wish to maintain in nurturing their children. It is always beneficial when both the parents adhere to a common standard of disciplining their children. Spouses must determine which of the child's behaviour are good and desirable and which are bad and undesirable. They must jointly determine the rules they want their children to follow. Once a standard is set, both the parents and the child must strictly abide.[5]

Learn to Adapt to the Change

It is always a joy to welcome a baby into one's home. At one point of time everything was shared just between the husband and the wife. They received undivided attention from each other. With the arrival of children, this scenario changes and this change may result in relationship crisis if it is not given proper attention. As children arrives one after the other, attention shared within the

---

[5] Lynn Clark, *SOS Help for Parents: A Practical Guide for Handling Common Everyday Behavior Problems*, 2nd ed. (Kentucky: Parents Press & SOS Programs), 2003.

spouse may be drastically reduced. It is not because they don't value each other anymore but it is due to the fact that their attention is diverted towards childcare. Depending on how one may take it, some relationship may disintegrate while some relationship will grow stronger during this phase. The two-way relationship shared between the husband and the wife has now turned into a three dimensional relationship between the father, mother and child. Parenting a child is strenuous for both parents yet one should not let the relationship between spouses go sour just because you have a child. They should also learn to adapt to the change in their relationship as a family which mean to say that they can no longer expect undivided attention from each other yet be ever willing to provide a healthy dose of attention to one another. The unwillingness to adapt to this change in relationship will prove to be quite disastrous for their relationship. Nurturing a child is important yet this task will be successful only when their relationship as husband and wife remain strong and healthy. "No matter how long a couple has been together, the marriage relationship has little chance of remaining healthy and vital if it takes a back seat to anything, if it tops in priority, every other relationship in life will be enriched."[6] One must never let the relationship between the spouses go cold just because a child arrived. This is a time when the strength of the bond they share as husband and wife is tested the most. Understanding one another, sacrificing one's comfort for the other, participating in child care etc. eases the strain of this period. For instance, the husband cannot sit in the corner and demand undivided attention while he does nothing to ease the burden of his wife in child care. He will definitely get nothing from his wife. Imagine the pressure of a spouse who juggle with his/her career as well as carry the burden of child nurturing and home management while the other half maintain passivity. Both spouses may be willing "to give and receive" if at all one is serious about their marital relationship. A high level of understanding is required from both parties. "To fail to understand one's spouse is to fail to

[6] Floyd and Harriet Thatcher, *Marriage for a Lifetime,* (Illinois: Harold Shaw Publishers, 1995), 161.

understand oneself. It is also a failure to grow and to fulfil one's possibility."[7] When the right adaptation happens, this is the phase when the bond between the spouses and the child grow stronger even with the shared attention they receive from one another.

[7] Paul Tournier, *To Understand Each Other,* (Atlanta: John Knox Press, 1967), 31.

Chapter 10

Partners in Parenting

"What you have started together, finish it together"

Rethinking the Traditional Concept of Role Play

Traditionally the task of child nurturing is attributed to be the responsibility of a mother. In fact, it is not just the nurturing of a child but managing the entire household too. The father is assigned the role of a bread earner. An evaluation of this traditional concept conceals an impression that has a strong influence in the way responsibilities is shared between a father and a mother today. Some people may argue that the reason for this distribution of role is as per the context of a particular time. It is undeniable that any study of a particular culture should always be done based on the context of a particular time and should not be consider just at the face value yet the bigger question to consider is the presence of the essence of such tradition in today's context which is misrepresented.

Have we allowed such cultural diktats as an excuse to shy away from our preordained responsibility? Check this illustration: A wife carrying a toddler on her back while trying to cook dinner for the family, the other kid throwing a tantrum in the corner while the husband sits cool beside the computer indulging in a game while sipping iced tea. Assuming that he has a job and returned from office certainly entitles him the traditional role of a bread earner but cannot be credited the entitlement of the role of a "partner in parenting." Both the husband and the wife are called to be partners in parenting and not just bread earners and home makers. There may be some parents who use cultural elements as cues to avoid certain responsibilities. If one parent gives up all the responsibility of caring for and bringing up children, both the parents and also the child lose out. One of the spouses carries an unfair burden and the other misses out the enriching life experience of partnering in raising their children. The child on the other hand loses the opportunity of bonding with the passive parent.[1] One's culture and tradition should be respected and the good elements must be adhered to but not at the expense of dodging one's preordained responsibility. Traditional concepts are based on their context and it was relevant for them in that particular context. In today's context the question of relevancy arises because of the change in times. The tradition of "fathers is the bread earner and mother the homemaker" also does not forbid us to share responsibility and become partners in raising the family. The distribution of role play is not rigid and it provides the opportunity to go beyond the prescribe role. Something that was relevant in a particular context may not be relevant today. We must be cautious and sensitive enough to understand the role each one of us should take up in parenting. We cannot just depend on culture and tradition but our instinct too. More than everything else parenting is instinctual. I believe one's instinct as a parent and a spouse should endow us the spirit to sacrifice all our comforts to share responsibilities and contribute ceaselessly towards nurturing our family in the right manner. The role play that is ascribed to the

[1] Mc Matthew, Anna Mathew and Beulah Wood, *Parenting Your Child*, (New Delhi: UBSPD, 2004), 4.

father and the mother should be reconsidered based on the context today.

The context today is way apart from the context a decade ago. A decade does not seem to be very far behind yet the change in lifestyle of the people is huge which should motivate us to perceive things from today's perspective. In today's world, it is common things to see both spouses employed and working outside of the home. It is no more the man's privilege alone to earn and sustain the family. In fact in many families, we notice women replacing the men as the bread earner. There are many families whose livelihood is completely dependent on the mother. Some couples with mutual understanding decide to switch the traditionally assigned roles. We see a shift in the conventionally assigned role play and It is imperative to check how parents should understand their role along with the change of time.

Parenting is Shared Responsibility

The task of nurturing a child should never be ascribed to be the sole responsibility of the mother. The concept of "your task, my task" should not arise in parenting because it is purely team work. The husband and the wife should belong to the same team not opposing teams. It starts with the simple conception of the child. Neither the husband not the wife by him/herself can conceive a child. They conceive the baby together but the role of either one does not stop there. They carry out the rest of the nurturing task together. The simple logic is, "What you have started together, finish it together." When the going gets tough, some may forget "we started it together." Whether it be parenting or any other tasks, it is never considered ethical to forsake our team and back off before seeing the task through.

God's blessing to Adam and Eve to be fruitful and multiply was directed to both equally. Gen. 1:28 records "God blessed them and said to them, be fruitful and multiply, and fill the earth and subdue it and have dominion over…" The act of being fruitful and multiplying is a team work. God did not intend Adam and Eve to just procreate but to multiply and fill the earth, subdue it and have dominion… A deeper look into this declaration of God reveals the call for a task that goes beyond procreation. No one appreciate a rotten apple and therefore "being fruitful" requires the children to be healthy fruits. "Multiplying and filling the earth" is not in terms of simply filling a bucket with water. It is about filling the created earth which required the children to be strategist. To "subdue and have dominion over God's creation" require tact and intelligence. Moreover, the children must recognize that the purpose of their life is to fulfil God's plan. These tasks will never be accomplished unless they are taught, nurtured, and disciplined well. This responsibility is ascribed by God to both parents. The impression of "two becoming one" in Gen. 2:24 sums it up. A married couple is no longer two individuals but one - a team. We cannot just procreate and leave the rest of the task to the other.

The Model of Compensation

God has created male and female equally but differently. They are created differently because they are meant to complement one another. This applies even in the task of child nurturing. For instance, from a physiological perspective only a woman is endowed with the ability to conceive, deliver a child, lactate naturally etc. This is one reason why some man think that child nurturing is a woman's thing. How feasible is the concept of partnership when we are not endowed with the ability to perform those tasks? The concept of partnership is misunderstood very often. Partnership does not require that the partners should be endowed with the same ability. In fact if the husband and the wife are endowed with the same ability, there is no point of convergence for them. They reason that they are together is because they are differently endowed gender based. There is a model which I like to term "the model of compensation." In another words it can also be termed as "compensating one's inability." What a husband and a wife can or cannot do gender based is something that need no explanation. The greater question is what a husband and a wife can do in areas where he/she cannot contribute as a partner. Since parenting is a partnership, one cannot just raise one's arm and surrender and leave the rest to the other half. Even in areas where we cannot contribute, there is always alternative ways of supporting one another.

A man will not be able to lactate naturally but he can compensate his inability by doing the laundry. A lactating mother may not sleep well at night and the husband can compensate by waking up early in the morning, do the household chores and let her sleep an extra hour or two. Even when one cannot do much, one can at least help the children finish their homework. When we apply the model of compensation, the task of child nurturing will be smooth and this truly complement one another. There is no question of "I can do this, I can't do this" when the model of compensation is applied in a marital relationship. This model not only applies to the task of child nurturing but this applies to the whole relationship between the husband and the wife. If there should be an illustration that helps simplify the model of compensation, it should go like this. It is the story of a young couple. The husband is a real gentleman but unfortunately lost his eyesight completely due to an accident; the wife is the sweetest among the two but has lost both her legs in the same accident involving her husband. The sweetest moment you will ever experience is when you come across this couple taking a "stroll" in the evening. The sweet lady sits on the wheelchair and behind her is the blind husband pushing the wheel chair slowly. The woman cannot walk but can see while the man can walk but cannot see. Knowing well that the husband cannot see, the wife narrates what she sees to her husband. She talks about the weather, the sunset, the people that they pass by and everything else that she sees. She makes her husband see with "her eyes." The husband with an occasional nod continues to push the wheelchair enjoying the 'vision" while allowing her to walk with "his legs." This story truly illustrates the model of compensation. The husband and the wife complemented one another and make themselves feel complete. As an individual both had their own inabilities but because of the act of complementing, they never let one another feel incomplete.

The Preordained Role of a Father/Mother: Gender Identity and Healthy Coexistence

No doubt, with the model of compensation they complement one another in the process of nurturing and raising a family. Yet, there are certain preordained roles only a mother/father can fulfil. Due to the fact that we are differently made, certain role fits only one of them the best. For instance the mother is endowed with the ability to conceive, give birth and lactate a child and this is a job which the husband cannot substitute. Similarly each parent has certain important role that cannot be substituted by the other. The biggest difference in the role of a mother and a father to their children is the need for their children to find a gender identity. A boy identifies himself with the father and a girl identifies herself with the mother.[2] This is a gender based role which cannot be replaced by another. Depending on how parents exhibit their role play, their children will develop the similar attitude towards the same as well as the opposite gender. The importance of the father –son relationship and how this bond is essential to masculine development is imperative.[3] A son learns what it means to be a male from his father. A girl similarly learns feminine traits from the mother. It is not just about learning and developing traits based on one's gender but children learn about healthy correlation with other gender from the other siblings as well as through the relationship shared between the mother and the father. Children pay particular attention to their father's reaction to the femininity of his daughters and they also pay attention to the father reaction to their mother's femininity. When the daughter sees that she is being ignored, the mother being mistreated or her brother getting all the attention, she develops inferiority complex as a female.[4] The issue of sex education also comes in. who can best talk about sex education to a son than the father and a mother to her daughter. I don't intend to justify that a father cannot teach her daughter or a mother to her son but I am focussing on the advantage of gender based sex education. For instance, a girl who has attained puberty will find it difficult to tell her father about the change

---

[2] Steve and Shaaron Biddulph, *Love, Laughter and Parenting,* (London: Dorling Kindersley, 2000), 168-170.

[3] James Dobson, *Bringing up Boys: Practical Advice and Encouragement for Those Shaping the Next Generation of Men,* (Illinois: Tyndale House Publishers, 2001), 56.

[4] James L. Schaller, *The Search for Lost Fathering: Rebuilding your Father's Relationship,* (Michigan: Fleming H. Revell, 1995), 43.

happening in her body; the mother suits this role best. A mother and her daughter share a special relationship because of their gender. Their feminine nature connects them from birth throughout life.[5] The same principle applies to a man and his son. This special bond as male and female should be appreciated and utilized the way it is meant to be.

Single Parenting

Parenting as a partnership does not imply anymore to single parents because of the circumstances they go through. Many people fall into this category not by choice but because of circumstances such as divorce, death of the spouse, abandonment by one of the spouses and so forth. Sometimes it is difficult to comprehend human destiny. Some people play with their destiny and ends up in a mess while some are destined to adversities. Some had the choice but some did not. For instance, in cases of pregnancy before marriage, they had the choice not to indulge in sex before marriage but ends up pregnant and later abandoned by the man. She ends up as a single mother if she chooses to give birth. Another instance where a person has no choice is the death of the spouse. After the death of the spouse the responsibility of the nurturing of the children falls on the shoulder of the other half. No matter the circumstances the simple fact is they ends up a single parent, burdened with the responsibility of nurturing a child/children. If parenting a child with the support of both parents is difficult, how are we going to measure the difficulty level of a single parent? If "partnership in parenting" applies to parenting involving both the father and the mother, what applies to a single parent? Is there a strategy that supports them in their endeavour as a single parent?

No matter the circumstances that let someone become a single parent, taking a step backward to revisit the initial stage is important. It is undeniable that the reason that they are parent though single now is because "they started it together" at one point of time. Retrace the simple logic of "what you have started together, finish it

---

[5] Rhonda H. Kelley, *Raising Moms,* (Alabama: New Hope Publishers, 2006), 39.

together." The only thing that differ now is one of them could not make it to the end. Remember that you have started as a team and in a battle, team members may fall but the one standing should never give up but fight until the end. You may be alone now but the team spirit remains with you and it is always a good feeling to know that you are representing a team. Therefore, the logic of "what you have started together, finish it together" applies to single parents too. The outcome of a soccer game is eventually credited to the team though someone in the team may score more and some none at all.

Single parents have a greater responsibility since they represents a team. Some single parents have given up struggling while many have brushed aside all hitches and with much pride represent the team which was established along with the husband/wife who is no more. The better half no more stands to support them in person yet he/she stands tall with the children waving the flag that represents their team so dear to his/her heart. Many innocent children have suffered and are suffering just because a single parent refused to hold the flag that represents their team. If we choose not to represent the team, it is okay but there is no excuse to escape ourselves from the responsibility of finishing what we have started already. Fate has made us single parent but our children do not deserve abandonment. Look out for resources available in the neighbourhood that extends emotional, spiritual and material support. Some single parent may be rich enough to sustain themselves but will definitely need spiritual and emotional support. Some may not need emotional and spiritual support but may need material support. Even when such resources are not available at hand, it is always wise to talk with the Pastor. The promise of God to sustain His people is not just a myth. He works in mysterious ways. People experience frustration and question the concept of God as the Provider. In fact there is nothing wrong with the concept; it is as clear as ever. The "wrong" is when we seek help from the wrong source. If we go to the right source for help, I am confident that help is at hand.

Chapter 11

The Grand Role of Grand Parenting

"Being a grandparent does not make you old and feeble"

Many people look forward to becoming grandparents and to be a grandparent is an accomplishment many don't achieve. If you are a grandparent today, remember that you are blessed. Along with the joy of witnessing your children grow and mature, what a joy to see your grandchildren and be a part of their nurturing. The Bible affirms this blessing in Pro. 17:6 which says, "Grandchildren are the crown of the aged, and the glory of children is their parents." Many people may consider this stage more from "aging" perspective but the trend today reveals that not all grandparents are old and feeble. Some may consider it from the perspective of "retirement" and "rest" which does not happen all the time. In fact the concept of getting old is underrated. Being old does not always mean the way we think it is. Ps. 92:12-14 beautifully portrays how the old people can still be youthful and productive. "The righteous flourishes like the palm tree...In old age they still produce fruit; they are still green and full of sap." We must although be careful about generalizing this concept because this reference states that it is the "righteous" who will continue to flourish like a palm tree and be fruitful even when old. God's gift for righteousness goes beyond human comprehension. From a human perspective, someone being youthful and productive in old age seems to be an intangible statement but the Bible affirms it and many who claimed this blessing proves to be living testimonies to us. Something that seems impossible becomes a reality to people who are rewarded for their righteousness by God. A reconsideration of the concept of being a grandparent is necessary. Like parenting itself, grandparenting is a gift, a reward from God. It affirms the blessing of longevity, continuation of the family's lineage and more importantly the grace of God. It is a reward as well as a responsibility. A "crown" over the head is not just a rewards but it involve being responsible and accountable to the one who crowned him/her.

Understanding Grandparent vs. Grandparenting

There are many grandparents today who are shouldering the complete responsibility of nurturing their grandkids due to factors such as death of the parents, divorce and so forth. Such circumstances forces grandchildren to end up at their grandparent's home. The entire fate depends on the nurturing of their grandparents. Some grandparents maintain their independence yet involve in the affairs of their children and grandchildren from a distance. Some grandparents may be completely dependent on their children, stay with them and become a part of them. Being a grandparent and grandparenting are two different things. The moment your children give birth to a child, you qualify to be a grandparent but grandparenting is when you continue to involve in the nurturing of your grandchildren either directly or from a distance, when you make you presence impact their lives and set a legacy for them. Many can become a grandparent yet many cannot engage in grandparenting. It is imperative for grandparents to understand the biblical mandate for grandparenting.

The Grand Role of Grandparents

1. Bridging the Gap

No parent is perfect and therefore, loopholes in parenting are a normal sight. Some identify it while some do not even know that there are loopholes being created in their parenting. The only person on earth who knows someone perfectly well is their parents, now grandparents of their children. Grandparents can therefore perfectly fill certain voids created between their children and their grandchildren. Grandparents are given by God to fill in the gaps missed by the grandchildren's parents.[1] This is a special role that every grandparent must look out for. When there is someone available to identify and fill the void created by us, what a privilege! For instance, when you notice that your grandkids are missing out on spiritual nurturing at home (no family fellowship, family prayer…); offer to take them to the church with you. When your grandkids miss the opportunity to spend quality time with their parents, your presence will be greatly beneficial for them.

2. Passing Over a Legacy

Ps. 71:18 has a clear call for grandparents towards grandparenting. The prayer of David goes like this. "So even to old age and grey hairs, O God do not forsake me, until I proclaim your might to all the generation to come…" When someone has experienced God intimately, he/she cannot just be satisfied by proclaiming about it to his/her generation alone. The quest to share it even with the next generation shall be sought. Grandparents have a major role to play in passing on a good legacy to their grandchildren. Ministry does not end as age advances. God is calling grandparents to be ministers of His divine love to the family.[2] Pro. 13:22 also has a direct reference to the role of grandparents leaving a good legacy behind. "The good leave an inheritance to their children's children…" The material inheritance you leave behind is fine but better to leave something

---

[1] Eric Wiggin, *The Gift of Grandparenting: Building Meaningful Relationship with Your Grandchildren,* (Illinois: Tyndale House Publishers, 2001), 204.

[2] Irene M. Endicott and C. Ferris Jordan, *Grandparenting by Grace,* (Nashville: Life Way Press, 1994), 32.

that will sustain their lives for eternity. Moses' sermon to the Israelites before entering the Promised Land included, "...do not forget the things that your eyes have seen nor to let them slip from your mind all the days of your life; make them known to your children and your children's children..." (Deut. 4:9). The responsibility of passing on the spiritual legacy not just to the present generation but to the next generation too is stressed in this sermon of Moses.

3. Create Lasting Memories for your Grandkids

The number of years I spend with my granddad is very few yet the memories of him, the enchanting stories he shared, the way he laugh, the pranks we played with him, the earnest prayer he said when any of his grandkids fall sick are all wonderful memories imprinted in my mind. As a grandparent, how do you want your grandkids to remember you after you are gone? What memories do you want them to hold on to? Remember that grandparents are "getting older" and they grandkids are "growing up." There is always a mystical connection between grandparents and grandkids. This connection enables the impression that you make upon the minds of your grandkids to remain super strong with them. Imagine people around us who never had "real moments" with one's parents, this relationship with the grandparents may be the only memories ever worth cherishing.

Deterrents for Grandparenting

1. The presence of a grandparent is always a welcoming sight to any grandkids. Their advices and parenting tips are respected and value yet each family will have to learn parenting traits by themselves and not just be dependent on others. Children who are married are no more kids and thus they should be given enough space to grow as a family. Learning how to nurture a family takes time and constant interference will make them dependant on the Grandparents for every affair in the family. Grandparents or any other members of the family intruding in all matter related to the family is not a healthy sign. There is a time to allow our children to spread their wings and fly. Give

your married children room to grow into their child-rearing responsibilities.[3] There are times when we just have to watch from a distance and allow them to grow as a family. Sometimes they may make mistake but it is okay as long as they learn from it. Your nurturing presence must be with them all the time yet it should not overpower their ability to decide and act on their own for the good of their family.

2. Grandparents may be tempted to go easy on their grandchildren and allow them to do anything they like. Grandparents may give them extra pocket money, pamper them too much, buy goodies excessively, and so forth. It is never with the intention to spoil them but an act of love yet from a parenting perspective; this may not be a good practice. As long as their parents maintain a standard set of do's and don'ts for their kid's discipline, one should be very careful not to meddle with it. The pampering received from the grandparents and the set of discipline they maintain at home may become a conflicting system and ultimately children or anyone else may prefer the pampering and hate the standard at home.
3. Disciplining of the grandkids must never be against the standard set by the parents. Even when the standard set by the parents is not satisfactory, grandparents must first discuss this with their children first and come to a common understanding. Without proper coordination, we may end up following contradicting system which will be quite confusing as well as amusing to the grandkids. This will also destroy our relationship with our own children. As long as parents have an achievable disciplinary standard for their kids, Grandparents must encourage their grandkids to adhere to the standard set by their parents and support the parent's effort to discipline their children.

---

[3] Eric Wiggin, *The Gift of Grandparenting: Building Meaningful Relationship with Your Grandchildren,* (Illinois: Tyndale House Publishers, 2001), 181.

Chapter 12

The Need for Pastoral Initiatives

"The church becomes real to people only when it deals with their real problems"

There is always a natural process of change happening with the family and it have to encounter and successfully complete the different phases of life. An effective pastoral care will make a big difference to assist parents to handle the important task of parenting in different phase of the life of the family. There are numerous issues that people are confronted with each day of their lives and for all these problems, the church is looked upon as a reservoir of solutions. Many people have now recognized that the church is a significant agent through which many changes can take place in the lives of individuals and society. The church can play a very positive role in nurturing a family that is whole. It starts with the preparation for marriage, sustaining the family within the church and community, and nurturing family life which is both ethical and pastoral. The pastoral care specialist can assist this process by making accessible the social skills and psychological insights helpful to it.

A clarion call for the churches to engage in a holistic ministry is proposed. The ministry of the churches should encompass all aspect of the human life. Issues related to parenting and childhood should be given due importance due to the fact that a family is a social unit of the society. The church/society is made up of smaller units which is the individual families. Each unit in turn builds up a strong community. Some sections of the society have no voice of their own and they suffer silently. Normally we choose to remain silent when the 'call for help' is faint and inaudible. In the similar way, we may tend to be a mute spectator to injustices being meted out to people who are the runt of the society. We do it because their cries are silenced by the noises of the dominant. The church is an epitome of justice, equality and righteousness. We cannot dare to ignore the silent cries of our people. We should make a move and consider it an integral part of the pastoral ministry.

Features of Pastoral Care

The five important functions of pastoral care are healing, sustaining, guiding, reconciling, and nurturing. The first three tasks viz, healing, sustaining and guiding are proposed by Seward Hiltner[1] and the reconciling task was the work of William A Clebsch and Charles R Jaekle[2] and the last task which is the nurturing task is the work of Howard Clinebell.[3] Pastoral care in the absence of these five elements is no pastoral care at all.

All these five elements are required for this aspect of ministry. For the subject we deal with in this book, these pastoral features fit in so well. A focussed elucidation about these five important pastoral features is exerted in the following.

---

[1] Seward Hiltner, *Preface to Pastoral Theology*, (Nashville: Abingdon Press, 1958), 89.

[2] William A Clebsch and Charles R. Jackle, *Pastoral Care in Historical Perspective*, New ed. (New York: Rowman & Littlefield Publishers, 1994), 9.

[3] Howard Clinebell, *Basic Types of Pastoral Care and Counselling*, (Nashville: Abingdon Press, 1984), 26.

Healing Ministry: Healing is the process of being restored to physical, emotional, mental and spiritual wholeness. Many families undergo brokenness and undergo immense pain and sorrow. The pastoral relationship shared with an individual/family may create the favourable environment for holistic healing to happen in their individual life and family. Sometimes individual's attempts to mend may result in more harm since everyone does know the process of restoring wholeness in their lives and family. The tendency to restrain from expressing their hurts in public also makes the matter worse and they try to suffer silently which affect their individual, familial and social life. The church is called to wipe the tears off the eyes of people who experiences brokenness and lead them towards healing of both the body and the soul. The process of healing the broken world begins when we heal the family.

Sustaining Ministry: Not every situation in life can change immediately with or without intervention. The ministry of sustaining steps into such situation and lend support and consolation. Situations such as death of a loved one, divorce, chronic sickness etc., mandate this form of ministry. It is a way of helping an individual cope with the current situation as he/she awaits full recovery. Sustaining ministry is important especially in situations when immediate help is not viable. People may lose hope and allow depression and other unhealthy mental state to set in leading to more complication such as suicides. There are cases everywhere where people resort to committing suicide because of issues related to the family. In the midst of conflict, helping them to sustain themselves until help arrives/issues settles down is very crucial. Normally people always expect immediate solutions to their problem and when their expectation is not met, it can be very depressing.

Guiding Ministry: The responsibility of a guide is immense. The church is called to guide people towards the right track. Some people consciously choose the wrong direction while some may go wrong because he/she does not know. In both the circumstances, the role of a guide becomes very important. People get married and start a family but not everyone has the ability to take their family in the right track. They constantly need the guiding hand of the church.

Guiding ministry also means helping an individual make the right and appropriate decisions in life. The illustration of a light house in the sea which helps the boats maintain their track even in the dark is the perfect example of this special ministry. The sighting of the light from the light house is an indication that they are not lost even when there is darkness everywhere.

Reconciling Ministry: In many homes, people struggle with strained relationship among the members. Strained relationship may be between the spouses, between parents and children and the in-laws and so on. In some cases, strained relationship may be between the family and God. Many go through it resulting in physical, emotional and spiritual harm not only to the individual but the whole members of the family. Any broken relationship both vertical and horizontal must be fixed immediately. These are moments in the life of individuals and families when we need someone/agencies to facilitate the reconciliation process. The involvement of a third party is always necessary in a reconciliation process and this can be fulfilled by the church through the reconciling ministry.

Nurturing Ministry: This is a ministry where individuals are helped to identify their potentials and nurtured. The analogy of a gardener can be beautifully illustrated to understand this aspect of pastoral care where he/she nurtures a plant from a small seed till it flowers and bear fruit. The seed by itself cannot accomplish it but the gardener helped the plant nurture itself into a full grown fruit bearing tree. There are many people with huge potentials but not nurtured well. Family too can be helped to nurture themselves into beautiful homes.

The Task of Safeguarding the Weak: A Christian Prerogative

The scripture has a substantial portion that instructs us to support and uplift the status of people who are weak. Psalms 82:1-4 is a clarion call to the people to defend the poor and the orphans, to be fair to the needy and the helpless and to rescue them from the hands of the wicked. Proverbs 31:8-9 encourages us to become the "Voice for the voiceless" and defend the right of the poor and needy. It is a Christian prerogative to support and voice out for people in need: children as well as anyone who needs support. James advocates certain norms of an undefiled religion and one of it is safeguarding the weak (James: 1:27). Jesus taught the rich people about including the poor in partaking their riches with the promise that the reward is great for them in the Kingdom of God (Luke 14:12-14). Defending the weak and voicing for the voiceless is a challenge that comes with the promise of a reward. Christianity as a religion is firmly based on the foundation of Love. The love we profess to the divine should be reciprocated in the way we deal with our fellow humans on earth. The heart of God is clear when it comes to aiding the needy and the poor; He expects his people to have the same heart for people around them who needs help and support.

1. Upgrade the Strategies of Children's Ministry

Churches should keep up with the trends and pace of the changing society and enhance the way we do children's ministry. A child today faces challenges completely different unlike the children some years ago. Children today have better knowledge of electronic gadgets, information, and technology than most adult. Their growth rate has literally shot up. We cannot continue to teach them like the way we have taught children in the past. Enhancing the way we do children's ministry today is a must.

> Children's ministry is like gardening where we cultivate, plant, and nurture the tender shoots of children's formative views of life and God. There are weeds, pests and diseases for which to watch out; but in the minds we are driven on by the hope of the fruit of our labour. Today the way we do gardening has changed because of the advancement of science and technology. Plants have become more resistant to diseases, grow faster and yield more.[4]

What the churches have done so far may have been relevant in the past but with the change of time, we need to upgrade the strategies

---

[4] Steve Alley, *Growing a Healthy Children's Ministry: A Step by Step Handbook to Cultivate Christian Kids in Any Environment* (Cincinnati: Standard Publishing, 2002), 6-7.

in line with the context. In many cases, children's ministry seems to be the most neglected among the other ministries of the church. The allocation of budget including the salary for this ministry is very meagre as compared to the other departments. In many churches, the Sunday school teachers are not trained enough to fit into the ministry. Sunday school or any other children's ministry should not be run like the conventional educational institutions and other Christian activities focussed at the adults. This should be definitely unique than the conventional institutions and this uniqueness is what should motivate our children towards developing themselves into matured Christians.

2. Upgrade the Strategies of the Church's Ministry

The church cannot afford to remain stagnant and monotonous in our approach while the world around us is moving ahead at a fast pace. Each family is an integral unit in the existence of the church. When the families are disintegrating, the church cannot just stay comfortable in her spiritual realm. Adequate parental impetus should be provided to parents as a part of the ministry of the church. Creating a proper ministerial framework for each church with assistance from experts will be the first step that each church can take up. A holistic approach towards creating a balanced ministerial framework is the need of the hour. The monotonous existence of the church should be revamped and the ministerial outlook should be in line with the change of time. The need of the people changes with the change of time. Similarly, the church should strive to become relevant to the need of the people.

3. Public Sensitization of Legal Issues

Taking into consideration the lack of awareness of the people towards legal issues and assistances, the church has a big role to play in sensitizing the minds of the people through networking with the right agencies. The church is always considered to be the best platform for educating people on varied issues and therefore, the church must consider sensitization of the general public on pertaining issues such as this. When sensitization happens starting from the grass root level, the level of harm upon the lives of children will be drastically reduced.

4. Enrich the Marriage

Marriage enrichment programs are designed to help couples make reasonably well functioning relationship even more mutually fulfilling.[5] The smooth functioning of the marriage is not only important just for the couple but it is of paramount importance for their children since their children's primary relationship and context will be the home. Enriching relationship shared between the husband and the wife will further be radiated into the lives of their kids. The two most important primary figures in a family are the husband and the wife. Nothing will seem right in the family when their relationship is not right. When relationship between spouses is not in good term, children are always at the receiving end. It is like the wave in the sea; one ripple creates another ripple. The church must design programs that should meet the need of people in all the stages of family life.

5. Enrich the Family

The task of family enrichment program is to meet the distinctive needs of couples, parents, and children as they move through the family life cycle. We must enrich family life by spiritual nurturing, developing interpersonal relationship, sharpening their focus on family concerns and create a healthy emotional environment leading to spiritual growth.[6] Family enrichment program is all about making families better. This is an area completely dedicated towards family life. It attempts to help family grow together in the Lord, maintain strong familial relationship with one another and sustain their family. Enough attention must be given towards this area and churches must seek professional help wherever required in framing the right modules in order that this becomes an integral part of the ministry of

---

[5] Howard Clinebell, *Basic Types of Pastoral Care and Counseling: Resources for the Ministry of Healing and Growth,* (Thiruvalla: Suvartha Bhavan, nd), 258.

[6] J. Clark Hensley, *The Pastor in Family Ministry,* (Mississippi: Family Ministry, 1990), 17.

the church. It should not be just a one-time event but framed in such a way that it becomes a regular part of the ministry of the church. This will materialize once we understand the importance of family in the life and ministry of the church. The church must involve in the developmental growth of each family.

6. Partner with Single Parent

Designing a special ministry that focuses on the need of the single parent in the church is a need of the hour. Most of the single parent undergoes problems related to finance, household management, emotional and spiritual frustration, custodial issues related to their children and many more. Ministry towards families, even when it exists are mostly confined towards conventional family of dual parenting and single parent families do not get the due attention. A special focussed attention to this group is required. Single parent families cannot be stereotyped. They need motivation, resources, and opportunities. These families can grow up to be viable, healthy growing families when the church is around to support them.[7] The need for the church to engage in programs that help them satisfactorily adapt to the role of a single parent is imminent.[8] Initiating a peer support group within the church/locality is also a big help since they understand what each member is going through and they will be able to render the right form of support to each other.

7. Empowering the Grandparents

The eleventh chapter of the book discussed on the grand role of grandparents and we have identified the importance of grandparents in nurturing their children's family, most particularly the grandchildren. A very special ministry is required that focuses on grandparents of our church and community. As discusses earlier, many grandparents may be stereotyped and made to consider

---

[7] Carolyn Koons, "Children of Single Parents," *Singles Ministry Handbook*, edited by Douglas L. Fagerstrom (Illinois: Victor Books, 1991), 65.

[8] John Kie Vining, *Effective Approaches to Family Ministry,* (New York: Cummings and Hathaway Publishers, 1995), 97.

themselves as useless and even a liability to the family. With right motivation, the presence of grandparents will prove to be a boon to the family particularly the grandchildren. Grandparents must be motivated towards positive living thereby helping them contribute towards the growth of their children's family. No matter how old they may be, they can live a productive life and contribute to the growth of the society in general. People should be taught to value the worth of grandparents and welcome their service towards the growth of the family.

8. Maintain a Uniform Standard

The church should be loud and clear towards the injustices that are happening to the children in our society. The church should not maintain a double standard nature where her clear voice is heard in some issues but choose to remain silent in some. The voice for justice and equality has been one of the strongest sermons of the church. When the church today is vocal in the subjects of interests and silent in regard to some issues, we cease to be the herald of justice and equality.

9. Say 'NO' to Child Domestic Labour

Most of our discussion and debates ends up mostly in the academic and professional level and it seldom reaches our homes. This is a sad fact about "high powered discussion." "Initiate a project that discourages the use of minors as helpers at home.[9] If necessary, use of adults as an extra hand should be encouraged that complies with the law of the land. Any form of arrangement between two parties that involve a child shall have to comply with the law of the land. Sometimes our goodwill efforts to help someone may turn out to be unethical and unlawful. The church should in fact collaborate with the local bodies/governmental agencies that monitor employment of minors and fight for the cause of the innocent children.

---

[9] This project will be successful only when Christian leaders say 'No' to the use of minors as helpers at one's own home. Many Christian leaders cannot muster enough courage to talk about issues related to children just because we ourselves have employed minors at home without adhering to the law of the land.

10. Pastoral Care and Counselling Training for Pastors

The nature of ministry the pastor engages with in this present context is immense. There was a time when someone who is zealous for church ministry took up pastoral role even without a formal theological training. Even today we see some people who responded to the call for pastoral ministry without undergoing theological training. Yet the need of the hour requires certain amount of formal training for the pastors. Even pastors who are theological trained must continue to be trained and refreshed. There should be provision for pastors both theological trained as well as others to undergo trainings and refreshers courses to equip them better towards an enhanced ministry. Counselling has become an important element of pastoral care and our pastors must be equipped with all tools possible in order that they perform better and be able to provide the right service to the people. With the change of time, people undergo new crisis in life. In most cases, pastors have to go beyond a simple prayer and a sermon and such cases require proper skill. Training our pastors and other church leaders is in fact an investment that every church must ungrudgingly invest.

11. Set Up a Counselling Cell

Setting up a counselling cell as a part of the ministry of the church has become a priority considering the nature of family problems that people faces today. Many of the pastors do not possess the right skill to provide counselling to the people in need. Similar to having departments for different categories of people such as the youth, women, children and so forth, we can consider having a counselling department too. Pastors should also be encouraged to pursue professional/short term trainings to enhance their counselling skills. A professional assistance from trained personnel may be required. A collaborated cell can also be managed by a group of churches where resources can be shared and utilized.

The ministerial framework of the church should be balanced. The voice of the church has always been given paramount importance by the people. The essence of this powerful voice should be used to right the wrong, lift up the weak and fight for the voiceless. No church should take up children's project just because this is the new ministerial trend but projects for children's welfare should be embraced because it is a sacred responsibility and the need of the hour. Many churches have the trend of following the program format of other organization without understanding the concept. We just copy what others do since it is the trend. Such attempts may not have a deep impact on people's lives unless we let the concept sink deep into our heart and minds and passionately strived towards extending a helping hand. We need to feel their pain by walking in their shoes. Anyone who has walked in the shoes of all those unfortunate children around us will never remain silent. Our silence silences the children's laughter and turns smile into frown. Every time we turn a blind eye to the plight of unprivileged people around us; we are silently encouraging the act. We may shut our eyes and pretend not to see evil around us and in the process we go blind forever. The deafening silence of people who can speak but remain mute; who see but choose to be blind is what is making human lose its human identity and particularly a Christian denigrate his Christian identity.

Conclusion

Parenting is no doubt a challenging responsibility. Viewing parenting from a Christian perspective makes it more significant because it is a divinely preordained obligation and hence is a call worth attending. The joy that transpire in a family in the form of children is something which cannot be expressed. The completeness one feels with the presence of our children at home is heavenly. I wish all parents get to know what it feels like to become parents in its whole sense. We should never let the weight of parenting drain away the privilege to fully immerse in the bliss of parenting. Along with the toil and tears involved in parenting, there is bliss. Christian parents must realize that parenting is not just a personal choice but it is a God's preordained obligation to nurture their children. A deeper understanding of the divine obligation as one take up parenting role is imperative to get the real taste of parenting. It is challenging but when we understand our call, we can take it in stride.

The responsibility of parenting will ease to a great extend when we have support from friends and family. Parents need help and this is a fact that should not be ignored. The greatest help we can possibly get can be derived from the bible, family and friends. Resources from the Bible, friends and family are a great boost for parenting. There are times when parents experience burnouts and receiving support from the right source will sustain us in accomplishing the task. The bible not only presents before us the biblical mandate but it also contains example of biblical parents who struggled like anyone of us. Some fared well while some did not. Such example prepares us towards maintaining the right strategy for parenting. Emulate the good examples and learn from the flaws committed by parents recorded in the pages of the Bible. Christian parenting cannot do away with the Bible and the guidebook for the task should be derived from the Bible. The norms of parenting basically depend on the culture that we adhere to and each culture dictates certain standards which are not applicable in all contexts. The solid foundation in which we can stand as parents is the biblical principles which are undoubtly relevant to all Christian parents irrespective of the culture and tradition one adheres to.

Disciplining children the right way is a question many parents ask but the answer to this question vary from culture to culture. The biblical mandate of disciplining our children with love holds a very powerful influence for today's parents. Disciplining is not just punishment for the wrong they might have done. Many parents just punish their children but fail to discipline them with love. Many parents punish their children because of their own uncontrolled anger and frustration which is not sanctioned by the scripture or another parenting guide book ever written. A thorough evaluation of how we discipline our kids is a must today. In the process of discipline we may end up 'breaking and distancing' them more if we are not cautious enough. Many parent-child relationships have been severed just because parents failed to understand how to discipline them the proper way.

Our children are our eternal possession. If we nurture them well they will follow us till heaven. We may forsake all our earthy possession one day but not our children. The only possession that we can consider our own eternally is our children. This though should ignite the enthusiasm to invest more into the nurturing and development of our children. We will not remain with them forever. When our time has come, we will pass away but the Christian legacy that we leave behind for them will sustain them even when we are gone. The spiritual nurturing that we invest in them will ultimately lead them to where we all should belong which is the eternal Heaven.

Parents must invest not just materially but most importantly spiritually and leave behind a solid spiritual legacy for their children to adopt.

The most important reason why many parents fail in their parental role is the lack of understanding a child's mind. We always look at them from the perspective of a parent. The irony is many forget that at one point of time we were also a child. The way children perceives and understand the adult world is completely different from the way an adult perceive. We cannot force them to look at this world from our viewpoint. Parents must educate themselves (not necessarily formal) to learn the worldview of a child and guide them likewise. Understanding a child's mind and dealing accordingly will ultimately ease a ton of stress parents may go through than just trying to have our own way upon a child.

Another aspect we must seriously consider is the relationship we share with our spouses. It has a direct impact upon the development of our children. Christian parenting is not just parent-child relationship but husband–wife relationship too. In the family the adult figure is represented by the father and the mother. In the family children learn about life in its complete sense. The relationship that children see being shared between the father and the mother is what they learn about human relationship. What we teach them verbally is secondary but the life we exhibit before them is what is primary for them. The language we use with one another, the love we express to one another, the care we show to one another are what they perceive to be whole.

If we have ever considered that this world do not have a darker side, we clearly know that it is a utopian dream. Beyond the perfection always lay gloom. A closer look at the perfect picture reveals a picture that is gross. The world appears to be free from hunger, the world appears to be child-friendly, education seems to be free, parenting seems to be easy but pictures of children around the world with no hope of a good future, parents in abject poverty with no prospect of educating their children, debauched people who take advantage of the poor and needy for their personal gain and comfort, the tears and utter helplessness on the face of children and parents are quite daunting. We are called to come out of our comfort zone and contribute towards helping the downtrodden and the needy. There are millions of children around the world who needs our help, there are parents around us struggling to sustain their family; struggling to discipline a wayward child. Don't turn a blind eye to the gloom in the faces. We may not be able to help millions but start by helping a child near you, start by helping a parent struggling near you. Never take advantage of people's misfortune. Today it may be their misfortune but tomorrow it may be ours.

No one survives by bread alone and this is what the Bible teaches us. We need something more than bread to survive. The holistic development of a person is what is required to live a complete life. Parents may provide food, education and shelter and consider their parenting role to be complete. In fact it is just a fraction of what is required from a parent. They need emotional, spiritual, physical support from parents. To people around you who need help, one can contribute support in all these areas. For those who are able to provide education, provide educational support. Those who cannot do so may provide emotional and spiritual support. Every ounce of help that you contribute is meaningful. The emphasis here is to declare that there should not be anyone who say "I cannot help" because everyone can contribute towards making this world a better place.

There is also a pastoral task that is involved which will supplement towards making Christian parenthood exciting as well as making this world a child-friendly world. The role of the church towards these causes must not be considered secondary but the ministry of the church should encompass all these aspects of human life. If there are churches who consider such aspect of ministry to be secondary to anything, I guess we are wrong. While the world weeps, the church cannot stay aloft and remain indifferent. The ministry of the church becomes real to people only when it deals with the real problems.

Bibliography

Aden, Leroy and J. Harold Ellens. eds. *The Church and Pastoral Care.* Grand Rapids: Baker Book House, 1988.

Alley, Steve. *Growing a Healthy Children's Ministry: A Step by Step Handbook to Cultivate Christian Kids in Any Environment.* Cincinnati: Standard Publishing, 2002.

Berk, Laura E. *Child Development.* Boston: Allyn and Bacon, 1989.

Bob and Ann Livesay. *Parenting Edition.* Nashville: Freeman-Smith, 2007.

Boyd, Charles F. *Different Children Different Needs: The Art of Adjustable Parenting.* Oregon: Multnomah Publishers, 1994.

Campbell, Ross. *How to Really Love Your Child.* Colorado: Life Journey, 2003.

Clark, Lynn. *SOS Help for Parents: A Practical Guide for Handling Common Everyday Behavior Problems*, 2nd ed. Kentucky: Parent Press & SOS Program, 2003.

Clinebell, Howard. *Basic Types of Pastoral Care and Counseling: Resources for the Ministry of Healing and Growth.* Rev. ed. Thiruvalla: Suvartha Bhavan, 2011.

________. *Basic Types of Pastoral Care and Counseling*. Nashville: Abingdon Press, 1984.

Deb, Sibnath. *Children in Agony: A Source Book.* New Delhi: Concept Publishing Company, 2006.

Dobson, James. *Bringing up Boys: Practical Advice and Encouragement for Those Shaping the Next generation of Men.* Illinois: Tyndale House Publishers, 2001.

Dobson, James. *The Strong Willed Child: Birth through Adolescence.* Illinois: Tyndale Publishers, 1984.

Donald, Cleveland Mc and Philip M. Mc Donald. *Creating a Successful Christian Marriage.* Michigan: Baker Books, 1994.

Endicott, Irene M and C. Ferris Jordan. *Grandparenting by Grace.* Nashville: Life Way Press, 1994.

Erikson, Erik. *The Life Cycle Completed.* Extended version. London: W.W. Norton & Company, 1997.

Fagerstrom, Douglas L (ed). *Singles Ministry Handbook.* Illinois: Victor Books, 1991.

Floyd and Harriet Thatcher. *Marriage for a Lifetime.* Illinois: Harold Shaw Publishers, 1995.

Hensley, J. Clark. *The Pastor in Family Ministry.* Mississippi: Family Ministry, 1990.

Hiltner, Seward. *Preface to Pastoral Theology.* Nashville: Abingdon Press, 1958.

Thorpe, Louis R. *Child Psychology and Development,* 2nd edition. New York: The Ronald Press Company, 1946.

Tournier, Paul. *The Adventure of Living.* New York: Harper and Row, 1965.

________. *To Understand Each Other.* Atlanta: John Knox Press, 1967.

Tom and Chaundel Holladay, *Love Powered Parenting,* Loving your Kids the way Jesus Loves You. Michigan: Zondervan, 2011.

Jones, Timothy. *Nurturing a Child's Soul.* Nashville: Word Publishing, 2000.

Kelley, Rhonda H. *Raising Moms.* Alabama: New Hope Publishers, 2006.

Kimmel, Tim. *Legacy of Love: A Plan for Parenting on Purpose*. Oregon: Multnomah Press, 1989.

Lasetso Razouselie, I. Toshi jamir and Woba James. *Nurturing Children in the Tribal Society of North East India: A Search for Values*. Jorhat: ILEMA, 2014.

Matthew, Mc, Anna Mathew and Beulah Wood, *Parenting Your Child*. New Delhi: UBSPD, 2004.

Narramore, Bruce. *Help! I'm a Parent*. Michigan: Zondervan Publishing House, 1972.

Paul D. Meier. *Christian Child–Rearing and Personality Development*. Michigan: Baker Book House, 1977.

Schaller, James L. *The Search for Lost Fathering: Rebuilding your Father's Relationship*. Michigan: Fleming H. Revell, 1995.

Spink, Kathryn. *Mother Teresa: An Authorized Biography*. London: Harper and Collins, 1997.

Steve and Shaaron Biddulph, *Love, Laughter and Parenting*. London: Dorling Kindersley, 2000.

Thakur, Lakshameshwar. *Child Development and Psychology*. New Delhi: Centrum Press, 2015.

Trent, John. Rick Osborne and Kurt Bruner. *Parents' Guide to the Spiritual Growth of Children: Helping Your Child Develop a Personal Faith*. Illinois: Tyndale House Publishers, 2000.

Vining, John Kie. *Effective Approaches to Family Ministry*. New York: Cummings and Hathaway Publishers, 1995.

Wiggin, Eric. *The Gift of Grandparenting: Building Meaningful Relationship with Your Grandchildren*. Illinois: Tyndale House Publishers, 2001.